The
Wiersbe
BIBLE STUDY SERIES

JOHN

The
Wiersbe
BIBLE STUDY SERIES

Get to Know

the Living

Savior

transforming lives together

THE WIERSBE BIBLE STUDY SERIES: JOHN
Published by David C Cook
4050 Lee Vance Drive
Colorado Springs, CO 80918 U.S.A.

David C Cook U.K., Kingsway Communications
Eastbourne, East Sussex BN23 6NT, England

The graphic circle C logo is a registered trademark of David C Cook.

All Scripture quotations in this study are taken from the *Holy Bible, New International
Version*®. *NIV*®. Copyright © 1973, 1978, 1984 by International
Bible Society. Used by permission of Zondervan. All rights reserved.

In the *Be Alive* and *Be Transformed* excerpts, all Scripture quotations, unless otherwise
noted, are taken from the King James Version of the Bible. (Public Domain.)
Scripture quotations marked NASB are taken from the *New American Standard Bible,*
© Copyright 1960, 1995 by The Lockman Foundation. Used by permission.

All excerpts taken from *Be Alive*, second edition, published by David C Cook in 2009 ©
1986 Warren W. Wiersbe, ISBN 978-1-4347-6736-3; and *Be Transformed,* second edition,
published by David C Cook in 2009 © 1986 Warren W. Wiersbe, ISBN 978-1-4347-6738-7.

ISBN 978-1-4347-6507-9
eISBN 978-0-7814-0490-7

© 2010 Warren W. Wiersbe

The Team: Steve Parolini, Karen Lee-Thorp, Amy Kiechlin,
Sarah Schultz, Jack Campbell, and Karen Athen
Cover Design: John Hamilton Design
Cover Photo: iStockphoto

Printed in the United States of America
First Edition 2010

9 10 11 12 13 14 15 16 17 18

110617

Contents

Introduction to John

The Theme

The gospel of John is simple enough for a child to wade in, but deep enough for the scholar and the most seasoned saint to swim in.

The basic theme of John's gospel is that Jesus Christ of Nazareth is the Son of God, and all who believe in Him receive eternal life (20:30–31). John's subject is the deity of Christ. John's object is to lead people into the life—eternal life, abundant life—that only Christ can give. John is both a theologian and an evangelist.

The Content

The first twelve chapters focus on our Lord's public ministry, especially the signs (miracles) that Jesus performed and the messages that grew out of some of them. The climax of His public ministry was official rejection by the religious rulers of Israel.

In chapters 13—21, John presents, for the most part, the private ministry of Christ with His own disciples. He was preparing them for their future service when the Holy Spirit would come and empower them. What the disciples experienced during those days completely transformed their lives.

Your Heart

Please come to this study with the heart and mind of a worshipper. John did not simply write a book; he painted exciting pictures. These pages are filled with images such as the Lamb, the door, the Shepherd, the new birth, the light and darkness, the Water of Life, bread, blindness, seeds, and dozens more. Use your "sanctified imagination" as you study, and the gospel of John will become a new book to you.

—*Warren W. Wiersbe*

How to Use This Study

This study is designed for both individual and small-group use. We've divided it into twelve lessons—each references one or more chapters in Warren W. Wiersbe's commentaries *Be Alive* and *Be Transformed* (second editions, David C. Cook, 2009). While reading the commentaries is not a prerequisite for going through this study, the additional insights and background Wiersbe offers can greatly enhance your study experience.

The Getting Started questions at the beginning of each lesson offer you an opportunity to record your first thoughts and reactions to the study text. This is an important step in the study process as those "first impressions" often include clues about what it is your heart is longing to discover.

The bulk of the study is found in the Going Deeper questions. These dive into the Bible text and, along with helpful excerpts from Wiersbe's commentary, help you examine not only the original context and meaning of the verses but also modern application.

Looking Inward narrows the focus down to your personal story. These intimate questions can be a bit uncomfortable at times, but don't shy away from honesty here. This is where you are asked to stand before the mirror of God's Word and look closely at what you see. It's the place to take a good look at yourself in light of the lesson and search for ways in which you can grow in faith.

Going Forward is the place where you can commit to paper those things you want or need to do in order to better live out the discoveries you made in the Looking Inward section. Don't skip or skim through this. Take the time to really consider what practical steps you might take to move closer to Christ. Then share your thoughts with a trusted friend who can act as an encourager and accountability partner.

Finally, there is a brief Seeking Help section to close the lesson. This is a reminder for you to invite God into your spiritual-growth process. If you choose to write out a prayer in this section, come back to it as you work through the lesson and continue to seek the Holy Spirit's guidance as you discover God's will for your life.

Tips for Small Groups

A small group is a dynamic thing. One week it might seem like a group of close-knit friends. The next it might seem more like a group of uncomfortable strangers. A small-group leader's role is to read these subtle changes and adjust the tone of the discussion accordingly.

Small groups need to be safe places for people to talk openly. It is through shared wrestling with difficult life issues that some of the greatest personal growth is discovered. But in order for the group to feel safe, participants need to know it's okay *not* to share sometimes. Always invite honest disclosure, but never force someone to speak if he or she isn't comfortable doing so. (A savvy leader will follow up later with a group member who isn't comfortable sharing in a group setting to see if a one-on-one discussion is more appropriate.)

Have volunteers take turns reading excerpts from Scripture or from the commentary. The more each person is involved even in the mundane tasks, the more they'll feel comfortable opening up in more meaningful ways.

The leader should watch the clock and keep the discussion moving. Sometimes there may be more Going Deeper questions than your group can cover in your available time. If you've had a fruitful discussion, it's okay to move on without finishing everything. And if you think the group is getting bogged down on a question or has taken off on a tangent, you can simply say, "Let's go on to question 5." Be sure to save at least ten to fifteen minutes for the Going Forward questions.

Finally, soak your group meetings in prayer—before you begin, during as needed, and always at the end of your time together.

God in the Flesh
(JOHN 1—2)

Before you begin ...
- *Pray for the Holy Spirit to reveal truth and wisdom as you go through this lesson.*
- *Read John 1—2. This lesson references chapters 1–2 in* Be Alive. *It will be helpful for you to have your Bible and a copy of the commentary available as you work through this lesson.*

Getting Started

From the Commentary

Much as our words reveal to others our hearts and minds, so Jesus Christ is God's "Word" to reveal His heart and mind to us. "He that hath seen me hath seen the Father" (John 14:9). A word is composed of letters, and Jesus Christ is "Alpha and Omega" (Rev. 1:11), the first and last letters of the Greek alphabet. According to Hebrews

1:1–3, Jesus Christ is God's *last* Word to mankind, for He is the climax of divine revelation.

—*Be Alive,* page 20

1. As you read John 1:1–2, what stands out to you about the description of "the Word"? What does it mean that the Word was "with" God? That the Word "was" God? How does this opening contrast with that of the other three gospel accounts (Matthew, Mark, and Luke)? What does this tell us about John, the writer of this gospel?

More to Consider: Why do you think John refers to Jesus as "the Son of God" so many times in his gospel? (See John 1:34, 49; 3:18; 5:25; 10:36; 11:4, 27; 19:7; 20:31.)

2. Choose one verse or phrase from John 1—2 that stands out to you. This could be something you're intrigued by, something that makes you uncomfortable, something that puzzles you, something that resonates with you, or just something you want to examine further. Write that here.

Going Deeper

From the Commentary

> *Life* is a key theme in John's gospel; it is used thirty-six
> times. What are the essentials for human life? There are
> at least four: light (if the sun went out, everything would
> die), air, water, and food. Jesus is all of these! He is the
> Light of Life and the Light of the World (John 8:12). He
> is the "Sun of righteousness" (Mal. 4:2). By His Holy
> Spirit, He gives us the "breath of life" (John 3:8; 20:22),
> as well as the Water of Life (John 4:10, 13–14; 7:37–39).
> Finally, Jesus is the Living Bread of Life that came down
> from heaven (John 6:35ff.). He not only has life and gives
> life, but He is life (John 14:6).
>
> —*Be Alive*, page 22

3. As you go through the gospel of John, underline the references to "life."
Why do you think John's gospel touches on this theme so frequently? How
do the themes of "light" and "life" relate to one another in John 1?

From the Commentary

> John the Baptist is one of the most important persons in
> the New Testament. He is mentioned at least eighty-nine
> times. John had the special privilege of introducing Jesus
> to the nation of Israel. He also had the difficult task of
> preparing the nation to receive its Messiah. He called
> them to repent of their sins and to prove that repentance
> by being baptized and then living changed lives. John
> summarized what John the Baptist had to say about Jesus
> Christ (John 1:15–18).
>
> —*Be Alive*, page 24

4. What is significant about the gospel writer's mention of John the Baptist
(John 1:6–28)? Why would this have been important to the early believers?

From Today's World

Although the skepticism of the modern age has diminished their impact,
self-proclaimed modern "prophets" continue to speak about the end of
the world (or other events) as if they have exclusive insight into "insider
information" from a source they often claim is God Himself. Some gain

a following as people clamor for wisdom about why the world is in its current state. Whether out of fear or frustration, they look to the so-called prophets for answers.

5. Why are people so fascinated (whether they agree or disagree) with modern prophets? Do you agree that people today are more skeptical about prophets and their reliability? Why or why not? How does today's culture compare to the culture in which John the Baptist appeared? What does this suggest about the role of prophecy in modern Christianity?

From the Commentary

The people of Israel were familiar with lambs for the sacrifices. At Passover, each family had to have a lamb, and during the year, two lambs a day were sacrificed at the temple altar, plus all the other lambs brought for personal sacrifices. Those lambs were brought by people to people, but here is God's Lamb, given by God to humankind! Those lambs could not take away sin, but the Lamb of God can take away sin. Those lambs were for Israel alone, but this Lamb would shed His blood for the whole world!

—*Be Alive*, pages 27–28

6. How might John's Jewish followers have responded when he announced Jesus as the "Lamb of God"? Why is John the Baptist's testimony important? How does John's description of the "Spirit" compare to the coming of the Holy Spirit as recorded in the book of Acts? What does this teach us about the Holy Spirit?

From the Commentary

"We have found the Messiah!" was the witness Andrew gave to Simon. *Messiah* is a Hebrew word that means "anointed," and the Greek equivalent is "Christ." To the Jews, it was the same as "Son of God" (see Matt. 26:63–64; Mark 14:61–62; Luke 22:67–70). In the Old Testament, prophets, priests, and kings were anointed and thereby set apart for special service. Kings were especially called "God's anointed" (1 Sam. 26:11; Ps. 89:20); so, when the Jews spoke about their Messiah, they were thinking of the king who would come to deliver them and establish the kingdom.

There was some confusion among the Jewish teachers as to what the Messiah would do. Some saw Him as a suffering sacrifice (as in Isa. 53), while others saw a splendid king (as in Isa. 9 and 11). Jesus had to explain even to His own followers that the cross had to come before the crown, that He must suffer before He could enter into His glory (Luke 24:13–35).

—*Be Alive*, page 29

7. Why were the Jews expecting the Messiah to appear as a king? What does this tell us about the culture and circumstance of the Jews at the time? How might the Jewish leaders have received the pronouncement of Jesus as the Messiah? There had been others who claimed messiahship prior to Jesus' arrival. What argument does John make in chapter 1 to support the fact that Jesus is the One they've been waiting for?

From the Commentary

"The third day" means three days after the call of Nathanael (John 1:45–51). Since that was the fourth day of the week recorded in John (John 1:19, 29, 35, 43), the wedding took place on "the seventh day" of this "new creation week." Throughout his gospel, John makes it clear that Jesus was on a divine schedule, obeying the will of the Father. Jewish tradition required that virgins be married on a Wednesday, while widows were married on a Thursday. Being the "seventh day" of John's special week, Jesus would be expected to rest, just as God rested on the seventh day (Gen. 2:1–3). But sin had interrupted God's Sabbath rest, and it was necessary for both the Father and the Son to work (John 5:17; 9:4). In fact, John recorded two specific miracles that Jesus deliberately performed on Sabbath days (John 5; 9). At this wedding, we see Jesus in three different roles: the Guest, the Son, and the Host.

—*Be Alive*, pages 35–36

8. Read John 2:1–11. Why do you think the Scriptures record this as Jesus' first miracle? What is the significance of turning water into wine? Of the timing of the miracle?

More to Consider: Moses' first miracle was a plague—turning water into blood (Ex. 7:19ff.), which speaks of judgment. How does Jesus' first miracle speak of grace?

From the Commentary

Jesus revealed His zeal for God first of all by *cleansing the temple* (John 2:13–17). The priests had established a lucrative business of exchanging foreign money for Jewish currency and also selling the animals needed for the sacrifices. No doubt, this "religious market" began as a convenience for the Jews who came long distances to worship in the temple, but in due time the "convenience" became a business, not a ministry. The tragedy is that this business was carried on in the court of the Gentiles in the temple, the place where the Jews should have been meeting the Gentiles and telling them about the one true God. Any Gentile searching for truth would not likely find it among the religious merchants in the temple.

—*Be Alive*, page 41

9. Why was Jesus so upset about the money changers? (See John 2:12–16.) What is significant about Jesus' comment in verse 19? How does this foreshadowing help us to see God's divine timetable for Jesus' earthly work?

From the Commentary

> While in Jerusalem for the Passover, Jesus performed
> miracles that are not given in detail in any of the Gospels.
> It must have been these signs that especially attracted
> Nicodemus (John 3:2). Because of the miracles, many
> people professed to believe in Him, but Jesus did not
> accept their profession. No matter what the people them-
> selves said or others said about them. He did not accept
> human testimony.
>
> *—Be Alive,* page 44

10. Why didn't Jesus accept human testimony? What does John mean
when he writes, "He did not need man's testimony about man, for he knew
what was in a man" (2:25)? What does this say about Jesus' feelings toward
those who followed Him because of His miracles?

Looking Inward

Take a moment to reflect on all that you've explored thus far in this study
of John 1—2. Review your notes and answers and think about how each
of these things matters in your life today.

Tips for Small Groups: To get the most out of this section, form pairs or trios and have group members take turns answering these questions. Be honest and as open as you can in this discussion, but most of all, be encouraging and supportive of others. Be sensitive to those who are going through particularly difficult times and don't press for people to speak if they're uncomfortable doing so.

11. How do you respond to the different descriptions of Jesus in John 1 (the Word, the Lamb, the Son of God)? In what ways does the father/son imagery connect with you? Why is it important for you to know Jesus was God's Son and not just a prophet sent to preach good news?

12. In what ways do you see your own life as a "light" to those around you? How have others been light to you? What are some ways you've struggled to be a light to others? How can the picture of Jesus as the light inspire you to be a light to others?

13. What sort of "Messiah" do you think you'd be hoping for if you were among the Jewish people before and during Jesus' time? In what ways might you have been pleasantly surprised by the way the Messiah arrived? In what ways might you have been disappointed? How do you see the Messiah's role in your life today? In what ways is Jesus' role like that of a king? Of a servant?

Going Forward

14. Think of one or two things that you have learned that you'd like to work on in the coming week. Remember that this is all about quality, not quantity. It's better to work on one specific area of life and do it well than to work on many and do poorly (or to be so overwhelmed that you simply don't try).

Do you want to know more about John's description of Jesus as "the Word"? Do you want to better understand the Jews' expectation about the

Messiah? Be specific. Go back through John 1—2 and put a star next to the phrase or verse that is most encouraging to you. Consider memorizing this verse.

Real-Life Application Ideas: John the Baptist contrasts his method of baptism with Jesus' in 1:26–34. How well do you know your church's stance on water baptism? Learn what your church teaches on this important topic. Consider what baptism has meant to you. Or, if you haven't yet been baptized, consider talking with your pastor about being baptized.

Seeking Help

15. Write a prayer below (or simply pray one in silence), inviting God to work on your mind and heart in those areas you've previously noted. Be honest about your desires and fears.

Notes for Small Groups:

- *Look for ways to put into practice the things you wrote in the Going Forward section. Talk with other group members about your ideas and commit to being accountable to one another.*

- *During the coming week, ask the Holy Spirit to continue to reveal truth to you from what you've read and studied.*

- *Before you start the next lesson, read John 3—4. For more in-depth lesson preparation, read chapters 3–4, "A Matter of Life and Death" and "The Bad Samaritan," in* Be Alive.

Life and Faith
(JOHN 3—4)

Before you begin ...
- *Pray for the Holy Spirit to reveal truth and wisdom as you go through this lesson.*
- *Read John 3—4. This lesson references chapters 3–4 in* Be Alive. *It will be helpful for you to have your Bible and a copy of the commentary available as you work through this lesson.*

Getting Started

From the Commentary

The new birth is one of the key topics in John 3. In addition, in this chapter we see Jesus Christ in three different roles: the Teacher (John 3:1–21), the Bridegroom (John 3:22–30), and the Witness (John 3:31–36).

—*Be Alive,* page 49

1. How is Jesus revealed in those three roles noted in John 3? How does each of these roles play into the overall theme of "new birth"?

More to Consider: What is the connection between John 2:23–25 and 3:1? What initially attracted Nicodemus to Jesus?

2. Choose one verse or phrase from John 3—4 that stands out to you. This could be something you're intrigued by, something that makes you uncomfortable, something that puzzles you, something that resonates with you, or just something you want to examine further. Write that here.

Going Deeper

From the Commentary

> In order to instruct Nicodemus in the basics of salvation, our Lord used four quite different illustrations: birth, wind, the serpent on the pole, and light and darkness.
>
> In John 3:1–7, our Lord began with that which was familiar, birth being a universal experience. The word translated "again" also means "from above." Though all human beings have experienced natural birth on earth, if they expect to go to heaven, they must experience a supernatural spiritual birth from above.
>
> Once again, we meet with the blindness of sinners: This well-educated religious leader, Nicodemus, did not understand what the Savior was talking about!
>
> —*Be Alive*, page 50

3. Why did Nicodemus have such a hard time understanding Jesus' meaning in John 3:3? In what ways is this misunderstanding typical of the hearts of those Jesus is attempting to teach? What are other examples from Scripture where Jesus was misunderstood? Why do you think Jesus taught using this method, rather than spelling out everything in great detail?

From the Commentary

> The word *wind* in both Hebrew and Greek can also be translated "spirit." One of the symbols of the Spirit of God in the Bible is the wind or breath (Job 33:4; John 20:22; Acts 2:2). Like the wind, the Spirit is invisible but powerful, and you cannot explain or predict the movements of the wind.
>
> When Jesus used this symbol, Nicodemus should have readily remembered Ezekiel 37:1–14. The prophet saw a valley full of dead bones, but when he prophesied to the wind, the Spirit came and gave the bones life. Again, it was the combination of the Spirit of God and the Word of God that gave life.
>
> —*Be Alive*, page 52

4. What makes the symbol of "wind" so appropriate to describe the Spirit? Read Ezekiel 37:1–14. How does this passage compare with the use of the symbol "wind" in John 3:8–13?

From Today's World

The term *born again* may have gained most of its popularity in Christian circles, but it has also become part of the common lexicon even outside of the church. When someone reinvents himself, others might refer to him as "born again." But because of Nicodemus's story, the term carries the most significance within the church. However, some Christians use the term in a way that can have a tendency to divide, rather than unite, believers. They hold it out as a differentiator between believers who have and haven't been "born again." According to John, however, if you are a Christ-follower, you are by definition born again.

5. Why do you think the term *born again* has negative connotations to some Christians (and non-Christians)? Why do people find it necessary to qualify believers as "born again" believers? What are they really asking? What does John 3 tell us about the significance of this phrase?

From the Commentary

> John the Baptist used a beautiful illustration. He compared Jesus to the bridegroom and himself only to the best man (John 3:29). Once the bridegroom and bride had been brought together, the work of the best man

was completed. What a foolish thing it would be for the best man to try to "upstage" the bridegroom and take his place. John's joy was to hear the voice of the Bridegroom and know that He had claimed His bride.

—*Be Alive*, page 56

6. Read John 3:27. What does John the Baptist mean by "A man can receive only what is given him from heaven." What was he given? What is his unique role in God's plan for salvation? How does that role compare with the role Christians have today to share the news about Christ?

From the Commentary

Because the Pharisees were trying to incite competition between Jesus and John the Baptist (John 3:25–30), Jesus left Judea and started north for Galilee. He could have taken one of three possible routes: along the coast, across the Jordan and up through Perea, or straight through Samaria. Orthodox Jews avoided Samaria because there was a long-standing, deep-seated hatred between them and the Samaritans.

The Samaritans were a mixed race, part Jew and part Gentile, that grew out of the Assyrian captivity of the ten northern tribes in 727 BC. Rejected by the Jews because they could not prove their genealogy, the Samaritans established their own temple and religious services on Mount Gerizim. This only fanned the fires of prejudice. So intense was their dislike of the Samaritans that some of the Pharisees prayed that no Samaritan would be raised in the resurrection! When His enemies wanted to call Jesus an insulting name, they called Him a Samaritan (John 8:48).

—*Be Alive*, pages 63–64

7. Read John 4:1–30. In what ways is it significant that Jesus left for Samaria right as the Pharisees were beginning to question His authority? Rather than "running away," Jesus found Himself in the middle of a controversial scene at the well with the Samaritan woman. What does this teach us about Jesus' mission? About God's "timetable" for presenting the gospel message to the world?

From the Commentary

> When the disciples returned from obtaining food, they were shocked that Jesus was conversing with a woman, and especially a Samaritan, but they did not interrupt. They were learning that their Master knew what He was doing and did not need their counsel. But, after the woman left, they urged Jesus to share the meal with them, because they knew that He was hungry.
>
> "I have meat to eat that ye know not of" was His reply, and, as usual, they did not understand it. They thought He was speaking of literal food, and they wondered where He got it. Then He explained that doing the Father's will—in this case, leading the woman to salvation—was true nourishment for His soul. The disciples were satisfied with bread, but He was satisfied with accomplishing the Father's work.
>
> —*Be Alive*, page 68

8. In what ways does Jesus feed the woman at the well? How does He feed His disciples after they return? What lesson did the disciples learn from Jesus' conversation with the woman?

More to Consider: Read Matthew 13:1–30; Romans 1:13; 1 Corinthians 3:6–9; and Galatians 6:9. How do these passages about the harvest shed light on the message of John 4:31–38?

From the Commentary

It is important that new converts be grounded in the Word—the Bible. These Samaritans began their spiritual walk by trusting in what the woman said, but they soon learned to trust the word taught by the Savior. Theirs was no "secondhand" salvation. They knew that they were saved because they had believed His message. "Now we know!" was their happy testimony.

You would have thought that these Samaritans would have been narrow in their faith, seeing Jesus as the Savior of the Jews and the Samaritans. But they declared that He was "the Savior of the world" (John 4:42). They had been converted only a few days, but they already had a missionary vision! In fact, their vision was wider than that of the apostles!

—*Be Alive*, pages 70–71

9. Read John 4:39–42. Why do you think the Samaritans were so quick to crown Jesus the Savior of the world and not just Savior of the Samaritans? What does this say about how they saw Jesus? About the power of one woman's testimony? About how our testimony today can influence others' lives?

From the Commentary

Why did Jesus return to Cana? Perhaps He wanted to cultivate the "seed" He had planted there when He attended the wedding feast. Nathanael came from Cana, so perhaps there was a personal reason for this visit. Jesus was met at Cana by a nobleman from Capernaum, some twenty miles away. The man had heard about His miracles and came all that distance to intercede for his son, who was dying. The first miracle at Cana came at the request of His mother (John 2:1–5), and this second miracle at Cana at the request of a father (John 4:47).

Was this man a Jew or a Gentile? We do not know. Nor do we know his exact position in the government. He may have been a member of Herod's court, but whatever his national or social standing, he was clearly at his wit's end and desperately needed the help of the Savior. He "kept beseeching him" to travel to Capernaum to heal his son.

—*Be Alive*, page 72

10. Read John 4:48–49. What is the point of Jesus' comment here? How does it speak to the condition of the people's hearts? In what ways does the official's response offer a contrast to what Jesus has just spoken? What does this section of Scripture teach us about miracles? About faith?

Looking Inward

Take a moment to reflect on all that you've explored thus far in this study of John 3—4. Review your notes and answers and think about how each of these things matters in your life today.

Tips for Small Groups: To get the most out of this section, form pairs or trios and have group members take turns answering these questions. Be honest and as open as you can in this discussion, but most of all, be encouraging and supportive of others. Be sensitive to those who are going through particularly difficult times and don't press for people to speak if they're uncomfortable doing so.

11. What does it mean to you to be "born again"? Does the phrase have positive connotations or negative ones? Explain. If you've been born again, is it important to use that phrase when telling other Christians about your faith? Why or why not?

12. What comes to mind when you think about the Holy Spirit? How is *wind* a fitting word picture of the Spirit? What questions do you have about the role of the Spirit in your life? How can you become more aware of and responsive to the Spirit?

13. In what ways are you like the Samaritan woman at the well? What are the things Jesus would say to you if He met you there? What "food" do you need from Jesus in order to be satisfied?

Going Forward

14. Think of one or two things that you have learned that you'd like to work on in the coming week. Remember that this is all about quality, not quantity. It's better to work on one specific area of life and do it well than to work on many and do poorly (or to be so overwhelmed that you simply don't try).

Do you need to respond to the wind of the Spirit? Be specific. Go back through John 3—4 and put a star next to the phrase or verse that is most encouraging to you. Consider memorizing this verse.

Real-Life Application Ideas: Take a survey of friends (both nonbelievers and believers), asking them to define the term born again. Then examine your results in light of John 3, and consider other ways to describe the same experience of becoming "new in Christ." What are some practical ways you can talk about being "new in Christ" with nonbeliever friends?

Seeking Help

15. Write a prayer below (or simply pray one in silence), inviting God to work on your mind and heart in those areas you've previously noted. Be honest about your desires and fears.

Notes for Small Groups:

- *Look for ways to put into practice the things you wrote in the Going Forward section. Talk with other group members about your ideas and commit to being accountable to one another.*

- *During the coming week, ask the Holy Spirit to continue to reveal truth to you from what you've read and studied.*

- *Before you start the next lesson, read John 5—6. For more in-depth lesson preparation, read chapters 5–6, "The Man Who Was Equal with God" and "Jesus Loses His Crowd," in* Be Alive.

Man of Miracles
(JOHN 5—6)

Before you begin ...
- *Pray for the Holy Spirit to reveal truth and wisdom as you go through this lesson.*
- *Read John 5—6. This lesson references chapters 5–6 in* Be Alive. *It will be helpful for you to have your Bible and a copy of the commentary available as you work through this lesson.*

Getting Started

From the Commentary

We do not know which feast Jesus was observing when He went to Jerusalem, and it is not important that we know. His main purpose for going was not to maintain a religious tradition but to heal a man and use the miracle as the basis for a message to the people. The miracle illustrated what He said in John 5:24—the power of His word and the gift of life.

—Be Alive, page 78

1. Why did Jesus ask the man at the well if he wanted to be healed (John 5:6)? What lesson did Jesus teach the observers of this miracle?

More to Consider: The Pool of Bethesda is situated near the northeast corner of the Old City, close to the Sheep Gate (Neh. 3:1; 12:39). What spiritual significance might this have had to the writer of the gospel of John?

2. Choose one verse or phrase from John 5—6 that stands out to you. This could be something you're intrigued by, something that makes you uncomfortable, something that puzzles you, something that resonates with you, or just something you want to examine further. Write that here.

Going Deeper

From the Commentary

> The miracle would have caused no problem except that it occurred on the Sabbath day. Our Lord certainly could have come a day earlier, or even waited a day, but He wanted to get the attention of the religious leaders. Later, He would deliberately heal a blind man on the Sabbath (John 9:1–14). The scribes had listed thirty-nine tasks that were prohibited on the Sabbath, and carrying a burden was one of them. Instead of rejoicing at the wonderful deliverance of the man, the religious leaders condemned him for carrying his bed and thereby breaking the law.
>
> —*Be Alive*, page 79

3. Why would miracles have been disallowed on the Sabbath, considering that the God of the Sabbath supposedly granted them? What does this tell us about the Jewish leaders' beliefs about God and the law? How did Jesus reframe their understanding of the law?

From the Commentary

Jesus made Himself equal with God because He is God. This is the theme of John's gospel. The Jewish leaders could not disprove His claims, so they tried to destroy Him and get Him out of the way. Both in His crucifixion and His resurrection, Jesus openly affirmed His deity and turned His enemies' weapons against them.

British writer George MacDonald pointed out that John 5:17 gives us a profound insight into our Lord's miracles. Jesus did *instantly* what the Father is always doing slowly. For example, in nature, as mentioned earlier, the Father is slowly turning water into wine, but Jesus did it instantly. Through the powers in nature, the Father is healing broken bodies, but Jesus healed them immediately. Nature is repeatedly multiplying bread, from sowing to harvest, but Jesus multiplied it instantly in His own hands.

—Be Alive, page 81

4. Respond to the following statement: "Jesus did *instantly* what the Father is always doing slowly." How is this implied or stated in John 5:17? How does this statement illustrate the connection between the Son and the Father? How does it help us to understand the point of Jesus' miracles?

From Today's World

The rules for the Sabbath included a whole host of things that weren't allowable on that day. This same sort of thinking led to what became known in America as the "blue laws," which prohibited such activities as the sale of alcoholic beverages or even all commerce all day Sunday or during certain hours. While most of these laws have been repealed, some remain (particularly the prohibition of alcohol sales in some states).

5. Why do you think American culture embraced the idea of the blue laws? What has changed in our culture that has resulted in the repealing of these laws? What value is there in restricting commerce on Sunday?

From the Commentary

John 5:21 certainly can mean much more than the physical raising of people from the dead, for certainly Jesus was referring to His gift of spiritual life to the spiritually dead. He amplified this truth further as recorded in John 5:24–29.

So, Jesus claimed to be equal with the Father in His works, but He also claimed to be equal with the Father in *executing judgment* (John 5:22). To the orthodox Jew, Jehovah God was "the Judge of all the earth" (Gen. 18:25), and no one dared to apply that august title to himself. But Jesus did! By claiming to be the Judge, He claimed to be God. "Because he [God] hath appointed a day, in the which he will judge the world in righteousness by that man whom he hath ordained" (Acts 17:31).

—Be Alive, page 83

6. Why does Jesus tell the people, "Do not be amazed at this" when claiming His authority as God's Son (5:28)? What is the significance of His statement that by Himself He can do nothing? What can believers today glean about judgment from the statement in John 5:30?

From the Commentary

Since John's gospel is selective (John 20:30–31), he does not record events in the life of Jesus that do not help him fulfill his purpose. Between the healing of the paralytic (John 5) and the feeding of the five thousand, you have many events taking place, some of which are mentioned in

Luke 6:1—9:10 and Mark 3:1—6:30. During this period our Lord preached the Sermon on the Mount (Matt. 5—7) and gave the parables of the kingdom (Matt. 13).

The feeding of the five thousand was a miracle of such magnitude that it is recorded in all four gospels. A great multitude had been following Jesus for several days, listening to His teaching and beholding His miracles. Jesus had tried to "get away" to rest, but the needs of the crowd pressed on Him (Mark 6:31–34). Because of His compassion, He ministered to the multitude in three different ways.

—Be Alive, page 93

7. If Jesus already had in His mind what He would do to feed the five thousand, why did He choose to test Philip? What do Philip's comments to Jesus reveal about him (6:5–7)? How does Andrew's response compare to Philip's? Why do you think it was important to note that there were leftovers after everyone was fed?

From the Commentary

> Jesus compelled the disciples to get into the boat (Matt. 14:22; Mark 6:45) because He knew they were in danger. The crowd was now aroused, and there was a movement to make Him King. Of course, some of the disciples would have rejoiced at the opportunity to become famous and powerful! Judas would have become treasurer of the kingdom, and perhaps Peter would have been named prime minister! But this was not in the plan of God, and Jesus broke up the meeting immediately. Certainly the Roman government would have stepped in had a movement begun.
>
> —*Be Alive*, page 95

8. Read John 6:14–15. How might the crowd have attempted to make Jesus King by force? Why would they want to do this? Are there any parallels to this ideology in today's church?

From the Commentary

> The disciples may have been impressed that so many people stayed through a storm in order to seek their Master, but Jesus was not impressed. He knows the human heart. He knew that the people originally followed Him because of His miracles (John 6:2), but now their motive was to get fed! Even if they were attracted only by the miracles, at least there was still a possibility they might be saved. After all, that is where Nicodemus started (John 3:1–2). But now their interest had degenerated to the level of food.
>
> Jesus pointed out that there are two kinds of food: food for the body, which is necessary but not the most important, and food for the inner man, the spirit, which is essential. What the people needed was not food but *life*, and life is a gift. Food only *sustains* life, but Jesus *gives* eternal life. The words of Isaiah come to mind: "Why do you spend money for what is not bread, and your wages for what does not satisfy?" (Isa. 55:2 NASB).
>
> —*Be Alive*, page 98

9. How does the response of the people to Jesus' miracle compare to the way people respond to the church today? In what ways does the church provide food for the hungry? How can providing for physical needs lead to a provision for spiritual needs? What does John 6:22–40 teach the church about reaching out to those with various needs?

From the Commentary

> Our Lord's messages recorded in the gospel of John are
> filled with symbolism and imagery. To take them literally
> is to make the same mistake the people made who first
> heard them.
>
> —*Be Alive*, page 104

10. Review the symbolism in John 6:48–59, and make a note of the
significant symbols. What is the meaning of each symbol? Why do people
often miss the point of symbolism in Scripture? What are the challenges in
interpreting these symbols? What role does the Holy Spirit play in helping
readers understand the symbolism in Scripture?

Looking Inward

Take a moment to reflect on all that you've explored thus far in this study
of John 5—6. Review your notes and answers and think about how each
of these things matters in your life today.

Tips for Small Groups: To get the most out of this section, form pairs or trios and have group members take turns answering these questions. Be honest and as open as you can in this discussion, but most of all, be encouraging and supportive of others. Be sensitive to those who are going through particularly difficult times and don't press for people to speak if they're uncomfortable doing so.

11. Think about things that cause you pain today (whether they're physical or emotional). How would you respond if Jesus asked you, "Do you want to be healed?" What would change in your life if you were healed from these painful circumstances? What might you learn if you are not healed?

12. Have you ever witnessed or experienced a miracle? If so, what was it? Why do you think there are fewer miracles today than in the time of the disciples? What purpose did the miracles play then? What purpose would they play today? If you know of someone who is in need of a miracle, take time to pray for that person.

13. What does the "bread of life" (6:35) mean to you? In what ways have you experienced the truth of this verse? In what ways have you longed to experience it? What does it mean to you that Jesus promises you'll never go hungry or be thirsty? What is He saying when He asks you to eat His flesh and drink His blood (6:53)?

Going Forward

14. Think of one or two things that you have learned that you'd like to work on in the coming week. Remember that this is all about quality, not quantity. It's better to work on one specific area of life and do it well than to work on many and do poorly (or to be so overwhelmed that you simply don't try).

Do you need to trust Jesus' power to heal or to feed? Do you want to further explore the symbolism in John's gospel? Be specific. Go back through John 5—6 and put a star next to the phrase or verse that is most encouraging to you. Consider memorizing this verse.

Real-Life Application Ideas: Jesus' miracle of the feeding of five thousand brought many people to a place where they could consider the spiritual food that God offers to all who seek Him. Consider organizing or participating in providing a meal for the homeless in your community. During this event, encourage people to explore the spiritual food offered in Scripture. Be sure to do this in a loving and undemanding way. The time should be one of discovery and opportunity for those who are led to seek more about God's truth.

Seeking Help

15. Write a prayer below (or simply pray one in silence), inviting God to work on your mind and heart in those areas you've previously noted. Be honest about your desires and fears.

Notes for Small Groups:

- *Look for ways to put into practice the things you wrote in the Going Forward section. Talk with other group members about your ideas and commit to being accountable to one another.*

- *During the coming week, ask the Holy Spirit to continue to reveal truth to you from what you've read and studied.*

- *Before you start the next lesson, read John 7—8. For more in-depth lesson preparation, read chapters 7–8, "Feast Fight" and "Contrasts and Conflicts," in* Be Alive.

Feast and Conflict
(JOHN 7—8)

Before you begin ...
- *Pray for the Holy Spirit to reveal truth and wisdom as you go through this lesson.*
- *Read John 7—8. This lesson references chapters 7–8 in* Be Alive. *It will be helpful for you to have your Bible and a copy of the commentary available as you work through this lesson.*

Getting Started

From the Commentary

Mary bore other children, with Joseph as their natural father (Matt. 13:55–56; Mark 6:1–6), so Jesus would have been their half brother. It seems incredible that His brothers could have lived with Him all those years and not realized the uniqueness of His person. Certainly they knew about His miracles (see John 7:3–4) since everybody else did. Having been in the closest contact with

Him, they had the best opportunity to watch Him and test Him, yet they were still unbelievers.

Here were men going up to a religious feast yet rejecting their own Messiah! How easy it is to follow tradition and miss eternal truth. The publicans and sinners were rejoicing at His message, but His own half brothers were making fun of Him.

—*Be Alive*, page 110

1. Read John 7:1–10. Why do you think Jesus' brothers suggested He become more public? What did they have to gain from Jesus' popularity? How is this like the way some people use God to further their own agendas?

More to Consider: Review John 2:4; 7:6, 8, 30; 8:20; 12:23; 13:1; 17:1. How do these passages illustrate the divine timetable God marked out for Jesus?

2. Choose one verse or phrase from John 7—8 that stands out to you. This could be something you're intrigued by, something that makes you

uncomfortable, something that puzzles you, something that resonates with you, or just something you want to examine further. Write that here.

Going Deeper

From the Commentary

> Note that this public debate about the Lord Jesus involved three different groups of people. First, of course, were the Jewish leaders ("the Jews") who lived in Jerusalem and were attached to the temple ministry. This would include the Pharisees and the chief priests (most of whom were Sadducees) as well as the scribes. These men differed theologically, but they agreed on one thing: their opposition to Jesus Christ and their determination to get rid of Him. The exceptions would be Nicodemus and Joseph of Arimathea (John 19:38–42).
>
> The second group would be "the people" (John 7:12, 20, 31–32). This would be the festival crowd that had come to Jerusalem to worship. Many of them would not be influenced by the attitude of the religious leaders at Jerusalem. You will note in John 7:20 that "the people" were amazed

that anybody would want to kill Jesus! They were not up to date on all the gossip in the city and had to learn the hard way that Jesus was considered a lawbreaker by the officials.

The third group was composed of the Jews who resided in Jerusalem (John 7:25). They, of course, would have likely sided with the religious leaders.

—*Be Alive*, page 112

3. Read John 7:11–36. What strikes you as the most compelling part of this discussion about Jesus? What is Jesus' response to the Jewish leaders? To the crowds? How is this diverse reaction to who Jesus is similar to the way people perceive Him today?

From the Commentary

Jesus explained that His doctrine came from the Father. He had already made it clear that He and the Father were one in the works that He performed (John 5:17) and in the judgment that He executed (John 5:30). Now He claimed that His teachings also came from the Father, and He would make that astounding claim again (John 8:26, 38). When I teach the Word of God, I can claim authority for the Bible but not for all of my interpretations of the Bible. Jesus rightly could claim absolute authority for everything that He taught!

—*Be Alive*, page 113

4. Read John 7:28–29. Couldn't any other religious teacher make a similar claim? How, then, can we know that Jesus was speaking the truth? What does it mean that "his time had not yet come" (v. 30)? What does this tell you about God's timetable for Jesus' story?

From the History Books

There have been more than a few people to claim they were the Messiah, including some who could easily be classified as crazy or insane. Despite their extreme claims and odd behaviors, some of these people (like David Koresh) still managed to collect at least a few followers who believed in them. Tragically, this also meant they were willing to die for the man they believed to be sent from God.

5. What prompts people to follow leaders with questionable intent or credentials? Why would the idea of a new messiah be appealing to some?

What are the clues that would help people see they're following not the true Messiah, but a counterfeit?

From the Commentary

> Water for drinking is one of the symbols of the Holy Spirit in the Bible. (Water for washing is a symbol of the Word of God; see John 15:3; Eph. 5:26.) Just as water satisfies thirst and produces fruitfulness, so the Spirit of God satisfies the inner person and enables us to bear fruit. At the feast, the Jews were reenacting a tradition that could never satisfy the heart. Jesus offered them living water and eternal satisfaction!
>
> —*Be Alive*, page 117

6. Read John 7:37–52. Why would Jesus speak about the Holy Spirit's role before the Spirit was poured out? How might the people have responded to this message? What surprises you about the responses to Jesus' message?

From the Commentary

> John 7:53—8:11 is not found in some of the ancient manuscripts; where it is found, it is not always in this location in John's gospel. Most scholars seem to agree that the passage is a part of inspired Scripture ("a fragment of authentic gospel material," says Dr. F. F. Bruce) regardless of where it is placed.
>
> To many of us, the story fits right here! In fact, the development of the entire chapter can easily be seen to grow out of this striking event in the temple. Our Lord's declaration on His being the Light of the World (John 8:12) certainly fits, and so do His words about true and false judgment (John 8:15–16, 26). The repeated phrase "die in your sins" (John 8:21, 24) would clearly relate to the judgment of the woman, and the fact that the chapter ends with an attempt to stone Jesus shows a perfect parallel to the opening story. The transition from John 7:52 to 8:12 would be too abrupt without a transitional section.
>
> —*Be Alive*, page 123

7. Why do you think this passage of Scripture (John 7:53—8:11) isn't found in some of the ancient manuscripts? Does this mean it is less valuable for us today? Why or why not? What lessons can we learn from the text?

From the Commentary

The Jewish leaders, of course, were trying to pin Jesus on the horns of a dilemma. If He said, "Yes, the woman must be stoned!" then what would happen to His reputation as the "friend of publicans and sinners"? The common people would no doubt have abandoned Him and would never have accepted His gracious message of forgiveness.

But, if He said, "No, the woman should not be stoned!" then He was openly breaking the law and subject to arrest. On more than one occasion, the religious leaders had tried to pit Jesus against Moses, and now they seemed to have the perfect challenge (see John 5:39–47; 6:32ff.; 7:40ff.).

—*Be Alive*, page 124

8. Did Jesus minimize the seriousness of adultery in 8:1–11? How can you tell? How does Jesus' treatment of this woman fit into the overall theme of His message to men and women? What does it mean to say that "forgiveness is free, but it is not cheap"?

More to Consider: Why do you think Jesus stooped to write on the ground when the Pharisees were questioning Him about the woman? Is it important that we know what He wrote? Why or why not? How might the Pharisees have perceived this simple act of writing in the sand?

From the Commentary

Jesus' second great "I am" statement (in John 8:12–20) fits into the context of the first eleven verses of John 8. Perhaps the sun was then appearing (John 8:2) so that Jesus was comparing Himself to the rising sun. But this would mean He was once again claiming to be God, for to the Jew, the sun was a symbol of Jehovah God (Ps. 84:11; Mal. 4:2). There is, for our galaxy, only one sun, and it is the center and the source of life. So there is but one God who is the center of all and the source of all life (John 1:4). "God is light" (1 John 1:5), and wherever the light shines, it reveals humanity's wickedness (Eph. 5:8–14).

—*Be Alive*, page 126

9. How does Jesus use the symbolism of "light" to claim He is God in John 8:12? How do the Pharisees react to this statement? What is your reaction to Jesus' answer in 8:14–18? Could this claim have been made by just anyone? If so, what makes Jesus' answer the truth?

From the Commentary

> Jesus had already mentioned His leaving them (John
> 7:34), but the Jews had misunderstood what He said.
> Once again, He warned them: He would leave them, they
> would not be able to follow Him, and they would die in
> their sins! They were wasting their God-given opportuni-
> ties by arguing with Him instead of trusting Him, and
> one day soon, their opportunities would end.
>
> Once again, the people misunderstood His teaching.
> They thought He was planning to kill Himself! Suicide
> was an abhorrent thing to a Jew, for the Jews were taught
> to honor all life. If Jesus committed suicide, then He
> would go to a place of judgment, and this, they reasoned,
> was why they could not follow Him.
>
> Actually, just the opposite was true: It was *they* who were
> going to the place of judgment!
>
> —*Be Alive*, page 128

10. Jesus states (in 8:21) that where He goes, "you cannot come." Why
might this have confused His followers? What did they expect from the
Messiah? How might this message (and the words that follow in chapter
8) have been misunderstood by those who were hearing Jesus speak? What
does this teach us about faith?

Looking Inward

Take a moment to reflect on all that you've explored thus far in this study of John 7—8. Review your notes and answers and think about how each of these things matters in your life today.

> *Tips for Small Groups: To get the most out of this section, form pairs or trios and have group members take turns answering these questions. Be honest and as open as you can in this discussion, but most of all, be encouraging and supportive of others. Be sensitive to those who are going through particularly difficult times and don't press for people to speak if they're uncomfortable doing so.*

11. Is it easy for you to believe Jesus is the Messiah? Why or why not? What evidence helps you to make your decision? What role does Scripture play in helping you to see who Jesus was and is? What role does the Holy Spirit play?

12. If you've ever been tempted to follow a leader other than Jesus, what led you to consider this? What caused you to question that leader? What is it about a leader that makes you want to follow? Where do you go to verify the integrity of a leader?

13. As you review Jesus' answers to the crowds and religious leaders in chapters 7 and 8, what is your immediate response to Jesus' claims about who He is? What doubts do you still have after reading this section of Scripture? What does this tell you about the role faith plays in knowing Christ?

Going Forward

14. Think of one or two things that you have learned that you'd like to work on in the coming week. Remember that this is all about quality, not quantity. It's better to work on one specific area of life and do it well than to work on many and do poorly (or to be so overwhelmed that you simply don't try).

Do you want to treat Jesus as the Light of the World? Do you want to turn your back on some area of sin? Be specific. Go back through John

7—8 and put a star next to the phrase or verse that is most encouraging to you. Consider memorizing this verse.

Real-Life Application Ideas: The message in John 8:1–11 is all about not judging others. Take inventory of the people in your life—at home, at work, at church. Have you been "casting stones" at any of these people in secret or in public? If so, what can you do to change your attitude or actions so they fall in line with what Jesus teaches about not judging others? If necessary, make plans to ask forgiveness for those you have wronged.

Seeking Help

15. Write a prayer below (or simply pray one in silence), inviting God to work on your mind and heart in those areas you've previously noted. Be honest about your desires and fears.

Notes for Small Groups:

- *Look for ways to put into practice the things you wrote in the Going Forward section. Talk with other group members about your ideas and commit to being accountable to one another.*

- *During the coming week, ask the Holy Spirit to continue to reveal truth to you from what you've read and studied.*

- *Before you start the next lesson, read John 9—10. For more in-depth lesson preparation, read chapters 9–10, "The Blind Man Calls Their Bluff" and "The Good Shepherd and His Sheep," in* Be Alive.

A Blind Man and the Shepherd
(JOHN 9—10)

Before you begin ...
- *Pray for the Holy Spirit to reveal truth and wisdom as you go through this lesson.*
- *Read John 9—10. This lesson references chapters 9–10 in* Be Alive. *It will be helpful for you to have your Bible and a copy of the commentary available as you work through this lesson.*

Getting Started

From the Commentary

Our Lord performed miracles in order to meet human needs. But He also used those miracles as a "launching pad" for a message conveying spiritual truth. Finally, His miracles were His "credentials" to prove that He was indeed the Messiah. "The blind receive their sight" was one such messianic miracle (Matt. 11:5), and we see it demonstrated in John 9.

—*Be Alive,* page 139

1. How does Jesus use the miracle in John 9 as a sermon on spiritual blindness? What is the message of this sermon? What lesson does Jesus teach from this same miracle in John 10?

More to Consider: Read Romans 5:12–21. What does this passage tell us about the source of physical problems? How does this passage in Scripture speak to the disciples' comments in John 9:1–12?

2. Choose one verse or phrase from John 9—10 that stands out to you. This could be something you're intrigued by, something that makes you uncomfortable, something that puzzles you, something that resonates with you, or just something you want to examine further. Write that here.

Going Deeper

From the Commentary

Since the Pharisees were the custodians of the faith, it was right that the healed man be brought to them for investigation. The fact that they studied this miracle in such detail is only further proof that Jesus did indeed heal the man. Since the man was *born* blind, the miracle was even greater, for blindness caused by sickness or injury might suddenly go away. Our Lord's miracles can bear careful scrutiny by His enemies.

But Jesus' act of deliberately healing the man on the Sabbath day caused the Pharisees great concern. It was illegal to work on the Sabbath; and by making the clay, applying the clay, and healing the man, Jesus had performed three unlawful "works." The Pharisees should have been praising God for a miracle; instead, they sought evidence to prosecute Jesus.

—*Be Alive*, pages 142–43

3. Why was it important for John to record the Pharisees' investigation of Jesus' healing miracle? Why would it have upset them? How does this piece of Jesus' story fit into the larger timeline God is orchestrating that will lead Him to the cross?

From the Commentary

> It seemed incredible to the healed man that the Pharisees
> would not know this Man who had opened his eyes! How
> many people were going around Jerusalem, opening the
> eyes of blind people? Instead of investigating the miracle,
> these religious leaders should have been investigating the
> One who did the miracle and learning from Him. The
> "experts" were rejecting the Stone that was sent to them
> (Acts 4:11).
>
> —*Be Alive*, page 146

4. Review John 9:24–34. Why did the Pharisees reject Jesus? Why did
they call Jesus a sinner? What theology lesson did the beggar give to the
Pharisees? How is the Pharisees' reaction like the reaction some people
have today to evidence of God's power?

From Today's World

In a culture where success is often met with suspicion, it seems there are
always people looking for "dirt" they can use to topple those who have
risen to the top. You see this, perhaps most vividly, in the political arena.

It has become an industry unto itself in the world of popular media, with Web sites and magazines dedicated solely to revealing the secrets and flaws of actors and musicians and others. And reporters are quick to jump on any story that purports to reveal a religious leader's sins or moral failure.

5. Why is our culture so fascinated with the flaws and failings of people who are in the public eye? Why are politicians, entertainers, and religious leaders often the targets of extra scrutiny? Is this deserved? How is the way people today seem eager to unseat leaders like the way the Pharisees were eager to discredit Jesus?

From the Commentary

Wherever Jesus went, some of the Pharisees tried to be present so they could catch Him in something He said or did. Seeing them, Jesus closed this episode by preaching a brief but penetrating sermon on spiritual blindness.

John 9:39 does not contradict John 3:16–17. The *reason* for our Lord's coming was salvation, but the *result* of His coming was condemnation of those who would not believe. The same sun that brings beauty out of the seeds also exposes the vermin hiding under the rocks.

The religious leaders were blind and would not admit it; therefore, the light of truth only made them blinder. The beggar admitted his need, and he received both physical sight and spiritual sight. No one is so blind as he who will not see, the one who thinks he has "all truth" and there is nothing more for him to learn (John 9:28, 34).

—*Be Alive*, pages 147–48

6. Why did the Pharisees take offense at Jesus' statement in John 9:39? In what ways were the Pharisees blind? What is the message of John 9:41? Where do you see this truth played out in today's Christian culture?

From the Commentary

John 10 focuses on the image of sheep, sheepfolds, and shepherds. It is a rural and Eastern image, to be sure, but it is an image that can say a great deal to us today, even in our urban, industrialized world. Paul used this image when admonishing the spiritual leaders in the church at Ephesus (Acts 20:28ff.). The truths that cluster around the image of the shepherd and the sheep are found throughout the Bible, and they are important to us today. The symbols that Jesus used help us understand who He is and what He wants to do for us.

—*Be Alive*, pages 153–54

7. How does the culture and context affect one's understanding of Jesus' message in John 10? Is it important to understand the agrarian culture of the time in order to understand Jesus' message? What modern analogies might express the same message today?

From the Commentary

Jesus opened His sermon with *a familiar illustration* (John 10:1–6), one that every listener would understand. The sheepfold was usually an enclosure made of rocks, with an opening for the door. The shepherd (or a porter) would guard the flock, or flocks, at night by lying across the opening. It was not unusual for several flocks to be sheltered together in the same fold. In the morning, the shepherds would come, call their sheep, and assemble their own flocks. Each sheep recognized its own master's voice.

The true shepherd comes in through the door, and the porter recognizes him. The thieves and robbers could never enter through the door, so they have to climb over the wall and enter the fold through deception. But even if they did get in, they would never get the sheep to follow them, for the sheep follow only the voice of their own shepherd. The false shepherds can never *lead* the sheep, so they must *steal* them away.

—*Be Alive*, pages 154–55

8. Go through John 10:1–10 and circle every mention of sheep. Why is "sheep" such a fitting image for this story? Why do you think the people didn't understand what Jesus was telling them (v. 6)? Who were those who "came before" Jesus (v. 8)? What does it mean that the sheep will find pasture?

From the Commentary

John 10:11–21 includes the fourth of our Lord's "I am" statements (John 6:35; 8:12; 10:9). Certainly in making this statement, He is contrasting Himself to the false shepherds who were in charge of the Jewish religion of that day. He had already called them "thieves and robbers," and now He would describe them as "hirelings."

The word translated "good" means "intrinsically good, beautiful, fair." It describes that which is the ideal, the model that others may safely imitate. Our Lord's goodness was inherent in His nature. To call Him "good" is the same as calling Him "God" (Mark 10:17–18).

—Be Alive, page 157

9. In what ways was Jesus acting as a shepherd during his early ministry (as you've been studying in this gospel)? Why did Jesus refer to the religious leaders of the time as "hired hands"? Review John 10:17. Why does Jesus include this explanation in the midst of a lesson on the Shepherd and the sheep?

From the Commentary

> The leaders surrounded Jesus in the temple so that He
> had to stop and listen to them. They had decided that it
> was time for a "showdown," and they did not want Him
> to evade the issue any longer. "How long are You going to
> hold us in suspense?" they kept saying to Him. "Tell us
> plainly—are You the Messiah?"
>
> Jesus reminded them of what He had already taught
> them. He emphasized the witness of His *words* ("I told
> you") and His *works* (see John 5:17ff. and 7:14ff. for simi-
> lar replies).
>
> —*Be Alive*, page 162

10. In what ways did Jesus reveal to the Jewish leaders that they didn't
understand His words? (See John 10:25–42.) Why were the leaders not
considered "sheep"? How does someone become one of the Shepherd's
sheep?

Looking Inward

Take a moment to reflect on all that you've explored thus far in this study of John 9—10. Review your notes and answers and think about how each of these things matters in your life today.

Tips for Small Groups: To get the most out of this section, form pairs or trios and have group members take turns answering these questions. Be honest and as open as you can in this discussion, but most of all, be encouraging and supportive of others. Be sensitive to those who are going through particularly difficult times and don't press for people to speak if they're uncomfortable doing so.

11. What surprised you most about the story of Jesus healing the blind man? Who do you relate to most in this story? The blind man? The Pharisees? Why? What can you take away from this story that can draw you closer to Christ?

12. Do you consider yourself a skeptic or a believer when it comes to healing? Explain your answer. If you need proof for things, how do you go about finding that proof? What role does faith play in your investigation of spiritual matters?

13. What is your response when leaders are put under a microscope by the media (and by other people in general)? Have you ever been in a similar situation? What are some of the good things that come from such scrutiny? What are some of the dangers?

Going Forward

14. Think of one or two things that you have learned that you'd like to work on in the coming week. Remember that this is all about quality, not quantity. It's better to work on one specific area of life and do it well than to work on many and do poorly (or to be so overwhelmed that you simply don't try).

Do you need to learn to trust Jesus as the Shepherd of your life? Do you want to investigate more about the claims of Christ? Be specific. Go back through John 9—10 and put a star next to the phrase or verse that is most encouraging to you. Consider memorizing this verse.

Real-Life Application Ideas: To grow in your understanding of John 10, do a study of sheep and shepherds in history and today. If you have an opportunity, talk with someone who shepherds a flock of sheep or other animals, or even spend time on a farm to experience a little piece of what Jesus was talking about.

Seeking Help

15. Write a prayer below (or simply pray one in silence), inviting God to work on your mind and heart in those areas you've previously noted. Be honest about your desires and fears.

Notes for Small Groups:

- *Look for ways to put into practice the things you wrote in the Going Forward section. Talk with other group members about your ideas and commit to being accountable to one another.*

- *During the coming week, ask the Holy Spirit to continue to reveal truth to you from what you've read and studied.*

- *Before you start the next lesson, read John 11—12. For more in-depth lesson preparation, read chapters 11–12, "The Last Miracle, the Last Enemy" and "Christ and the Crisis," in* Be Alive.

Crisis
(JOHN 11—12)

Before you begin ...
- *Pray for the Holy Spirit to reveal truth and wisdom as you go through this lesson.*
- *Read John 11—12. This lesson references chapters 11–12 in* Be Alive. *It will be helpful for you to have your Bible and a copy of the commentary available as you work through this lesson.*

Getting Started

From the Commentary

The raising of Lazarus from the dead was not our Lord's last miracle before the cross, but it was certainly His greatest and the one that aroused the most response from both His friends and His enemies. John selected this miracle as the seventh in the series recorded in his book because it was really the climactic miracle of our Lord's earthly ministry. He had raised others from the dead, but

Lazarus had been in the grave four days. It was a miracle that could not be denied or avoided by the Jewish leaders.

If Jesus Christ can do nothing about death, then whatever else He can do amounts to nothing. "If in this life only we have hope in Christ, we are of all men most miserable" (1 Cor. 15:19). Death is man's last enemy (1 Cor. 15:26), but Jesus Christ has defeated this horrible enemy totally and permanently.

—Be Alive, page 169

1. What are the main themes in John 11? Respond to the following statement: "If Jesus Christ can do nothing about death, then whatever else He can do amounts to nothing." How does Jesus' resurrection of Lazarus speak to this statement?

More to Consider: Jesus was at Bethabara, about twenty miles from Bethany (John 1:28; 10:40) when He got the news that Lazarus was sick. That's a one-day trip if traveling quickly. How might the messenger have felt when Jesus merely sent back an encouraging message rather than racing to Lazarus's side? How is this similar to the expectations Christians have today when it comes to sickness and God's possible healing power?

2. Choose one verse or phrase from John 11—12 that stands out to you. This could be something you're intrigued by, something that makes you uncomfortable, something that puzzles you, something that resonates with you, or just something you want to examine further. Write that here.

Going Deeper

From the Commentary

> God's love for His own is not a pampering love; it is a perfecting love. The fact that He loves us and we love Him is no guarantee that we will be sheltered from the problems and pains of life. After all, the Father loves His Son, and yet the Father permitted His beloved Son to drink the cup of sorrow and experience the shame and pain of the cross. We must never think that love and suffering are incompatible. Certainly they unite in Jesus Christ.
>
> —*Be Alive*, page 171

3. As you read the story of Lazarus, what emotions do you experience? In what ways is this story an example of "perfecting love" instead of "pampering love"? How did Jesus use this incident as an opportunity to glorify God? What does this tell us about the importance of glorifying God? About the relative importance of having a comfortable life?

From the Commentary

When our Lord announced that He was returning to Judea, His disciples were alarmed, because they knew how dangerous it would be. (Bethany is only about two miles from Jerusalem.) But Jesus was willing to lay down His life for His friends (John 15:13). He knew that His return to Judea and the miracle of raising Lazarus would precipitate His own arrest and death.

—*Be Alive*, page 172

4. How did Jesus calm the disciples' fears when He told them He was returning to Judea? (See John 11:7–10.) In what ways was this another reminder of the timetable the Father had given Jesus? (See John 2:4; 7:6, 8,

30; 8:20; 12:23; 13:1; 17:1.) In what ways did the disciples misunderstand the schedule—and also the reason for Jesus' visit to Lazarus?

From the Commentary

> Perhaps the greatest transformation Jesus performed was to move the doctrine of the resurrection out of the future and into the present. Martha was looking to the future, knowing that Lazarus would rise again and that she would see him. Her friends were looking to the past and saying, "He could have prevented Lazarus from dying" (John 11:37)! But Jesus tried to center their attention on the *present:* Wherever He is, God's resurrection power is available *now* (Rom. 6:4; Gal. 2:20; Phil. 3:10).
>
> —*Be Alive*, page 175

5. In what ways did Jesus' resurrection of Lazarus help to prepare His disciples for His own death and resurrection? What other lessons did this experience teach the disciples? What can we learn from Martha's conversation with Jesus (John 11:21–27)? From Mary's conversation (vv. 28–34)?

From the Commentary

> Our Lord's weeping reveals the humanity of the Savior.
> He has entered into all of our experiences and knows
> how we feel. In fact, being the perfect God-man, Jesus
> experienced these things in a deeper way than we do. His
> tears also assure us of His sympathy; He is indeed "a man
> of sorrows and acquainted with grief" (Isa. 53:3). Today,
> He is our merciful and faithful High Priest, and we may
> come to the throne of grace and find all the gracious help
> that we need (Heb. 4:14–16).

> We see in His tears the tragedy of sin but also the glory
> of heaven. Perhaps Jesus was weeping *for* Lazarus, as well
> as *with* the sisters, because He knew He was calling His
> friend from heaven and back into a wicked world where
> he would one day have to die again. Jesus had come down
> from heaven; He knew what Lazarus was leaving behind.
> —*Be Alive*, page 177

6. What do you think was the initial reaction to Jesus' tears? Why might
the spectators have thought He was crying? What does this say about their
belief in Jesus' healing power? How is today's church like or unlike the
spectators in this story?

More to Consider: Read Ephesians 2:1–10. How does the experience of Lazarus illustrate what happens to a sinner when he trusts Jesus?

From the Commentary

When she came to the feet of Jesus, Mary took the place of a slave. When she undid her hair (something Jewish women did not do in public), she humbled herself and laid her glory at His feet (see 1 Cor. 11:15). Of course, she was misunderstood and criticized, but that is what usually happens when somebody gives his or her best to the Lord.

—*Be Alive*, page 185

7. Review John 12:1–11. Why is it significant that Judas began the criticism of the woman who anointed Jesus? How might the other disciples have received Judas's comment? What is the point of Jesus' statement that "you will always have the poor among you, but you will not always have me"? What does this say about Jesus' concern for the poor? About the timetable His Father had Him on?

From the Commentary

> John shifted the scene from a quiet dinner in Bethany
> to a noisy public parade in Jerusalem. All four gospels
> record this event, and their accounts should be compared.
> This was the only "public demonstration" that our Lord
> allowed while He was ministering on earth.... The result
> was a growing animosity on the part of the religious lead-
> ers, leading eventually to the crucifixion of the Savior.
>
> There were three different groups in the crowd that day:
> (1) the Passover visitors from outside Judea (John 12:12,
> 18); (2) the local people who had witnessed the raising
> of Lazarus (John 12:17); and (3) the religious leaders
> who were greatly concerned about what Jesus might do
> at the feast (John 12:19). At each of the different feasts,
> the people were in keen expectation, wondering if Jesus
> would be there and what He would do.
>
> —*Be Alive*, page 187

8. Read John 12:12–19 and Zechariah 9:9. Why did Jesus allow this
particular public demonstration? Why did it result in more animosity
from the religious leaders? Why was the manner in which Jesus fulfilled
prophecy such a bone of contention for the religious leaders?

From Today's World

Jealousy has been chewing away at relationships since the fall. Today, it is at the root of many failures in relationships and businesses. It's a popular theme in movies and certainly a familiar topic for gossip magazines. With the rise of interest in social media sites, jealousy is taking on a whole new level of significance as people notice and then wonder "who is that?" when looking at a spouse's "friends" or "followers" list, which often includes old high school friends and even former boy- or girlfriends.

9. How is the jealousy that people deal with today similar to what the Pharisees might have felt as they watched Jesus gain a following? Why is jealousy such a dangerous thing? How can we combat jealousy?

From the Commentary

The central theme of this message is the glory of God (John 12:23, 28). We would have expected Jesus to say, "The hour is come, that the Son of man should be crucified." But Jesus saw beyond the cross to the glory that would follow (see Luke 24:26; Heb. 12:2). In fact, the glory of God is an important theme in the remaining chapters of John's gospel (see John 13:31–32; 14:13; 17:1, 4–5, 22, 24).

Jesus used the image of a seed to illustrate the great spiritual truth that there can be no glory without suffering, no fruitful life without death, no victory without surrender. Of itself, a seed is weak and useless; but when it is planted, it "dies" and becomes fruitful. There is both beauty and bounty when a seed "dies" and fulfills its purpose. If a seed could talk, it would no doubt complain about being put into the cold, dark earth. But the only way it can achieve its goal is by being planted.

—Be Alive, page 191

10. What is the suffering that Jesus was referring to in John 12:27? How might the disciples have interpreted this? What does this entire section of chapter 12 (vv. 20–36) teach us about the relationship between suffering and glory? In what ways are God's children like seeds? (See 12:23–26.)

Looking Inward

Take a moment to reflect on all that you've explored thus far in this study of John 11—12. Review your notes and answers and think about how each of these things matters in your life today.

Tips for Small Groups: To get the most out of this section, form pairs or trios and have group members take turns answering these questions. Be honest and as open as you can in this discussion, but most of all, be encouraging and supportive of others. Be sensitive to those who are going through particularly difficult times and don't press for people to speak if they're uncomfortable doing so.

11. What are some ways you've experienced God's perfecting love? What sort of suffering have you endured (or are you enduring) that you believe is an example of God's love? Is it easier to endure hard times knowing God is in control? Explain.

12. Are you more like Mary or Martha in your approach to Jesus? Why do you think this is true? What are the good things about being like Mary? Like Martha?

13. In John 12:25, Jesus says, "The man who loves his life will lose it, while the man who hates his life in this world will keep it for eternal life." What does this mean to you? What does it look like, practically speaking, to "hate your life" in this world?

Going Forward

14. Think of one or two things that you have learned that you'd like to work on in the coming week. Remember that this is all about quality, not quantity. It's better to work on one specific area of life and do it well than to work on many and do poorly (or to be so overwhelmed that you simply don't try).

Do you need to trust God's timing? Do you need to learn how to better endure suffering so that God can teach you through it? Be specific.

Go back through John 11—12 and put a star next to the phrase or verse that is most encouraging to you. Consider memorizing this verse.

Real-Life Application Ideas: The anointing of Jesus at Bethany made a powerful point about the importance of honoring God's timing (in this case, the brief time His Son would be on this earth). Think about the ways you honor God's timing in your own life. What are some things you're doing now that illustrate your desire to glorify God for His plan, for the schedule He has you on in life? If you tend to focus more on tasks than God's love, what can you do to be more present in the moments God gives you? Come up with some practical ways you can offer an "anointing" time to God.

Seeking Help

15. Write a prayer below (or simply pray one in silence), inviting God to work on your mind and heart in those areas you've previously noted. Be honest about your desires and fears.

Notes for Small Groups:

- *Look for ways to put into practice the things you wrote in the Going Forward section. Talk with other group members about your ideas and commit to being accountable to one another.*

- *During the coming week, ask the Holy Spirit to continue to reveal truth to you from what you've read and studied.*

- *Before you start the next lesson, read John 13—14. For more in-depth lesson preparation, read chapters 1–2, "The Sovereign Servant" and "Heart Trouble" in* Be Transformed.

Humility and Heart

(JOHN 13—14)

Before you begin …

- *Pray for the Holy Spirit to reveal truth and wisdom as you go through this lesson.*
- *Read John 13—14. This lesson references chapters 1–2 in* Be Transformed. *It will be helpful for you to have your Bible and a copy of the commentary available as you work through this lesson.*

Getting Started

From the Commentary

Jesus had entered Jerusalem on Sunday and on Monday had cleansed the temple. Tuesday was a day of conflict as the religious leaders sought to trip Him up and get evidence to arrest Him. These events are recorded in Matthew 21—25. Wednesday was probably a day of rest, but on Thursday He met in the upper room with His disciples in order to observe Passover.

The emphasis in John 13:1–3 is on *what our Lord knew,* and in John 13:4–5 on *what our Lord did.* Jesus knew that "his hour was come." More than any of the gospel writers, John emphasized the fact that Jesus lived on a "heavenly timetable" as He did the Father's will. Note the development of this theme:

2:4—"Mine hour is not yet come."

7:30—"His hour was not yet come."

8:20—"His hour was not yet come."

12:23—"The hour is come, that the Son of man should be glorified."

13:1—"Jesus knew that his hour was come."

17:1—"Father, the hour is come."

—*Be Transformed*, page 18

1. Review the passages listed above. What does this "heavenly timetable" tell us about God? About Jesus' closeness with His Father? About the disciples' understanding of Jesus' purpose?

More to Consider: Jesus knew that Judas would betray Him, and yet He didn't say anything to the other disciples. What does this tell us about Jesus' understanding of His own timetable and about the closeness between Jesus and His Father in heaven?

2. Choose one verse or phrase from John 13—14 that stands out to you. This could be something you're intrigued by, something that makes you uncomfortable, something that puzzles you, something that resonates with you, or just something you want to examine further. Write that here.

Going Deeper

From the Commentary

> The Father had put all things into the Son's hands, *yet Jesus picked up a towel and a basin!* His humility was not born of poverty, but of riches. He was rich, yet He became poor (2 Cor. 8:9). A Malay proverb says, "The fuller the ear is of rice-grain, the lower it bends."

It is remarkable how the gospel of John reveals the humility of our Lord even while magnifying His deity: "The Son can do nothing of himself " (John 5:19, 30). "For I came down from heaven, not to do mine own will" (John 6:38). "My doctrine is not mine" (John 7:16). "And I seek not mine own glory" (John 8:50). "The word which ye hear is not mine" (John 14:24). His ultimate expression of humility was His death on the cross.

—*Be Transformed*, page 20

3. Why was it important at this point in Jesus' story to express humility to the disciples? What was the disciples' response? What is the meaning behind Jesus' statement in John 13:16 that "no servant is greater than his master, nor is a messenger greater than the one who sent him"?

More to Consider: Contrast John 13:1 with 1:11 and 3:16. What does this contrast tell us about why Jesus served His disciples?

From the Commentary

Peter did not understand what his Lord was doing, but instead of waiting for an explanation, he impulsively tried to tell the Lord what to do. There is a strong double negative in John 13:8. The Greek scholar Kenneth Wuest translated Peter's statement, "You shall by no means wash my feet, no, never" (WUEST). Peter really meant it! Then when he discovered that to refuse the Lord would mean to lose the Lord's fellowship, he went in the opposite direction and asked for a complete bath!

—*Be Transformed*, page 22

4. What is the positive result of Peter's impulsive behavior in John 13:6–11? What is the negative result? How did Peter adjust his response after Jesus spoke (v. 8–9)? What can Peter's behavior teach us about responding to the things God asks of us?

From Today's World

Servant leadership has become a popular form of leadership in recent years. Whereas in the past many businesses preferred a management model that elevated leaders above the rest of the employees, some of the more successful businesses in the current economy are led by men and women who practice servanthood in one form or another. This is especially true of companies that place a high value on customer service and customer interaction.

5. What are the risks inherent in leading with a servant's heart? What are the benefits? What can Jesus' serving heart teach leaders today about taking care of the people who work for them? In what ways does this model of leadership run against the grain?

From the Commentary

John 13:17 is the key to understanding John 13:12–17— "If ye know these things, happy are ye if ye do them." The sequence is important: humbleness, holiness, then happiness. Aristotle defined happiness as "good fortune joined to virtue ... a life that is both agreeable and secure." That might do for a philosopher, but it will never do for a Christian believer! Happiness is the by-product of a life that is lived in the will of God. When we humbly serve

others, walk in God's paths of holiness, and do what He
tells us, then we will enjoy happiness.

—*Be Transformed*, page 23

6. Why does Jesus ask His disciples if they understand what He's done
for them (John 13:12)? How does Jesus redefine the role of teacher by His
act of foot-washing? In what ways will the disciples (and subsequently, all
believers) be blessed if they do as Jesus has done?

From the Commentary

John 13:36—14:31 opens and closes with our Lord's loving admonition, "Let not your heart be troubled" (John
14:1, 27). We are not surprised that the apostles were
troubled. After all, Jesus had announced that one of them
was a traitor, and then He warned Peter that he was going
to deny his Lord three times. Self-confident Peter was
certain that he could not only follow his Lord, but even
die with Him and for Him. Alas, Peter did not know his
own heart, nor do we really know *our* hearts, except for
one thing: Our hearts easily become troubled.

Perhaps the heaviest blow of all was the realization that Jesus was going to leave them (John 13:33).

—*Be Transformed*, page 33

7. What sorts of questions would have been prompted by Jesus' announcement that He was leaving (John 13:33)? Right after announcing His imminent departure, Jesus gives the disciples a new command, but Peter seems distracted by Jesus' mention of His leaving. What prompts Peter's question in John 13:37? How does Jesus respond to Peter?

From the Commentary

John 14:3 is a clear promise of our Lord's return for His people. Some will go to heaven through the valley of the shadow of death, but those who are alive when Jesus returns will *never* see death (John 11:25–26). They will be changed to be like Christ and will go to heaven (1 Thess. 4:13–18).

Thomas's question revealed his keen desire to be with Jesus (see John 11:16), and this meant that he had to know where the Master was going and how he himself would get there. The Lord made it clear that He was going to the Father, and that He was the only way to the Father. Heaven is a real place, a loving place, and an exclusive place. Not everybody is going to heaven, but rather only those who have trusted Jesus Christ (see Acts 4:12; 1 Tim. 2:4–6).

—*Be Transformed*, page 35

8. Jesus comforts the disciples in John 14:1–4. How might the disciples have misinterpreted His comforting words? Why does Jesus say, "You know the way to the place where I am going" (v. 4)? What is the way He's referring to?

More to Consider: Four hundred years before Christ was born, the Greek philosopher Plato wrote, "To find out the Father and Maker of all this universe is a hard task, and when we have found Him, to speak of Him to all men is impossible." How does Jesus' life, death, and resurrection prove Plato wrong?

From the Commentary

> "Why pray when you can worry?" asks a plaque that I have seen in many homes. One of the best remedies for a troubled heart is prayer.
>
> O what peace we often forfeit,
>
> O what needless pain we bear;
>
> All because we do not carry
>
> Everything to God in prayer.
>
> However, if God is going to answer our prayers and give us peace in our hearts, there are certain conditions that we must meet. In fact, the meeting of these conditions is a blessing in itself!
>
> —*Be Transformed*, page 38

9. Read John 14:12–15. What are the conditions we must meet in order for God to answer our prayers? How is meeting those conditions a blessing?

From the Commentary

The Holy Spirit abides in the believer. He is a gift from the Father in answer to the prayer of the Son. During His earthly ministry, Jesus had guided, guarded, and taught His disciples, but now He was going to leave them. The Spirit of God would come to them *and dwell in them,* taking the place of their Master. Jesus called the Spirit "another Comforter," and the Greek word translated "another" means "another of the same kind." The Spirit of God is not different from the Son of God, for both are God. The Spirit of God had dwelt *with* the disciples in the person of Jesus Christ. Now He would dwell *in* them.

Of course, the Spirit of God had been on earth before. He empowered men and women in the Old Testament to accomplish God's work. However, during the Old Testament Age, the Spirit of God would come on people and then leave them. God's Spirit departed from King Saul (1 Sam. 16:14; 18:12), and David, when confessing his sin, asked that the Spirit not be taken from him (Ps. 51:11). When the Holy Spirit was given at Pentecost, He was given to God's people to remain with them forever. Even though we may grieve the Spirit, He will not leave us.

The way we treat the Holy Spirit is the way we treat the Lord Jesus Christ.

—*Be Transformed,* page 41

10. How might the disciples have responded to Jesus' promise of the Holy Spirit? Why do you think Jesus referred to the Holy Spirit as "Counselor" (John 14:26)? Circle the times Jesus uses the word *peace* in John 14:27. Why might this have been important for the disciples to hear? Why is it still important for Christians today?

Looking Inward

Take a moment to reflect on all that you've explored thus far in this study of John 13—14. Review your notes and answers and think about how each of these things matters in your life today.

> *Tips for Small Groups: To get the most out of this section, form pairs or trios and have group members take turns answering these questions. Be honest and as open as you can in this discussion, but most of all, be encouraging and supportive of others. Be sensitive to those who are going through particularly difficult times and don't press for people to speak if they're uncomfortable doing so.*

11. As you consider the timeline Jesus had in His story, what does this tell you about God's hand in history? How do you see God's hand in your own history? In your current story? How can you know what path you're

supposed to take in life? What resources do you search to know what God's plan is for you?

12. When have you served others? When have others served you? What makes serving difficult? What makes it easy? If you are uncomfortable serving, what steps can you take so you can grow more comfortable with it?

13. John 3:12–17 illustrates a path to happiness. How does this match up with your own experience? What role does humility play in your happiness? What role does holiness play?

Going Forward

14. Think of one or two things that you have learned that you'd like to work on in the coming week. Remember that this is all about quality, not quantity. It's better to work on one specific area of life and do it well than to work on many and do poorly (or to be so overwhelmed that you simply don't try).

Do you want to understand more about being a good servant? Be specific. Go back through John 13—14 and put a star next to the phrase or verse that is most encouraging to you. Consider memorizing this verse.

Real-Life Application Ideas: Arrange a foot-washing service and practice what Jesus teaches. You can do this with a small group or even with your family. Be sure to include the reading of John 13:1–17 in your service. Afterward, talk about the experience with participants and look for practical applications to everyday life.

Seeking Help

15. Write a prayer below (or simply pray one in silence), inviting God to work on your mind and heart in those areas you've previously noted. Be honest about your desires and fears.

Notes for Small Groups:

- *Look for ways to put into practice the things you wrote in the Going Forward section. Talk with other group members about your ideas and commit to being accountable to one another.*

- *During the coming week, ask the Holy Spirit to continue to reveal truth to you from what you've read and studied.*

- *Before you start the next lesson, read John 15:1— 16:16. For more in-depth lesson preparation, read chapters 3–4, "Relationships and Responsibilities" and "What in the World Is the Spirit Doing?" in* Be Transformed.

Relationships
(JOHN 15:1—16:16)

Before you begin ...
- *Pray for the Holy Spirit to reveal truth and wisdom as you go through this lesson.*
- *Read John 15:1—16:16. This lesson references chapters 3–4 in* Be Transformed. *It will be helpful for you to have your Bible and a copy of the commentary available as you work through this lesson.*

Getting Started

From the Commentary

The cultivation of vineyards was important to the life and economy of Israel. A golden vine adorned Herod's temple. When our Lord used this image, He was not introducing something new; it was familiar to every Jew. There are four elements in this allegory that we must understand to benefit from His teaching.

1. The vine

2. The branches

3. The vinedresser

4. The fruit

—*Be Transformed,* pages 49–53

1. Go through John 15:1–17 and circle all the references to the vine, branches, vinedresser, and fruit. What does each of these elements represent? How do they work together to make Jesus' point?

More to Consider: The word abide *is used several times in John 15:1–11 (KJV). What does it mean to "abide"? Why is this word so important to the message of John 15?*

2. Choose one verse or phrase from John 15:1—16:16 that stands out to you. This could be something you're intrigued by, something that makes you uncomfortable, something that puzzles you, something that resonates with you, or just something you want to examine further. Write that here.

Going Deeper

From the Commentary

> Most of us have many acquaintances but very few friends, and even some of our friends may prove unfriendly or even unfaithful. What about Judas? "Yes, mine own familiar friend, in whom I trusted, which did eat of my bread, hath lifted up his heel against me" (Ps. 41:9). Even a devoted friend may fail us when we need him most. Peter, James, and John went to sleep in the garden when they should have been praying, and Peter even denied the Lord three times. Our friendship to each other and to the Lord is not perfect, but His friendship to us is perfect.
>
> However, we must not interpret this word *friend* in a limited way, because the Greek word means "a friend at court." It describes that "inner circle" around a king or emperor. (In John 3:29, it refers to the "best man" at a wedding.) The "friends of the king" would be close to him and know his secrets, but they would also be subject to him and have to obey his commands. There is thus no conflict between being a friend and being a servant.
>
> —*Be Transformed*, pages 55–56

3. Review John 15:12–17. What does Jesus mean when He says, "I no longer call you servants, because a servant does not know his master's business"? What is the "master's business" Jesus is referring to? How does the message of John 15:16 apply to each believer today?

From the Commentary

Our friendship with Christ involves love and obedience. But it also involves knowledge: He "lets us in on" His plans. Indeed, He is our Master (John 13:13, 16), but He does not treat us as servants. He treats us as friends, *if* we do what He commands. Abraham was God's friend because he obeyed God (Gen. 18:19). If we have friendship with the world, we then experience enmity with God (James 4:1–4). Lot in Sodom was not called God's friend, even though Lot was a saved man (2 Peter 2:7). God told Abraham what He planned to do to the cities of the plain, and Abraham was able to intercede for Lot and his family.

It is interesting to note that, in John's gospel, it was the servants who knew what was going on! The servants at the wedding feast in Cana knew where the wine came from (John 2:9), and the nobleman's servants knew when the son was healed (John 4:51–53).

One of the greatest privileges we have as His friends is that of learning to know God better and "getting in on" God's secrets.

—*Be Transformed*, page 57

4. In John 15:15, Jesus tells His disciples, "Everything that I learned from my Father I have made known to you." What does this tell us about the importance of knowing God? How do we get to know God better?

From the Commentary

John 15:18—16:16 is tied together by two important themes: the opposition of the world against the church, and the ministry of the Spirit to and through the church. Our Lord had been talking about love (John 15:9–13, 17), but now He is talking about *hatred,* and He used the word seven times. It seems incredible that anyone would hate Jesus Christ and His people, but that is exactly what the situation is today, and *some of that hatred comes from religious people.* In a few hours, the religious leaders of Israel would be condemning their Messiah and crying out for His blood.

Throughout the gospel of John, it is evident that the religious establishment not only opposed Jesus, but even sought to kill Him (John 5:16; 7:19, 25; 8:37, 59; 9:22; also note 11:8). As He continued His ministry, there was a tide of resentment, then hatred, and then open opposition toward Him. So, the disciples should not have been surprised when Jesus brought up the subject of persecution, for they had heard Him warn them and they had seen Him face men's hatred during His ministry.

—*Be Transformed,* pages 63–64

5. Read Matthew 5:10–12, 44; 10:16–23; and 23:34–35. What do these verses tell us about the inevitability of persecution? Why was there so much hatred of Jesus? How does that hatred trickle down to believers today? (See John 16:18–25.) What should our response be to that persecution?

From Today's World

While American Christians have enjoyed the freedom to practice their faith freely, there are still places around the globe where Christians are persecuted and even killed for practicing their faith. And yet, they continue to practice, even in the face of danger. In China, churches that aren't officially sanctioned by the government are shut down and members are imprisoned. Christians in India are often the target of more violent attacks.

6. Why does persecution of Christians continue today? What should our response be to the challenges faced by Christians in countries that aren't friendly toward Christianity? What are some ways Christians are persecuted even in America? What does Jesus have to say to those who are persecuted?

From the Commentary

Jesus pulls no punches when He tells His disciples that their situation in the world will be serious and even dangerous. Note the progress in the world's opposition: hatred (John 15:18–19), persecution (John 15:20), excommunication, and even death (John 16:2). You can trace these stages of resistance as you read the book of Acts.

—*Be Transformed*, page 65

7. According to John 15:18—16:4, why does the world hate Christians? Why does Jesus warn the disciples about persecution? (See John 16:4.) How does this truth apply to Christians around the globe today?

From the Commentary

Jesus emphasized His words and His works in John 15:22–24; 16:1–4. We have seen this emphasis throughout the gospel of John (3:2; 5:36–38; 10:24–27; 14:10–11). The people had no excuse ("cloak") for their sin. They had seen His works and heard His word, but they would not admit the truth. All of the evidence had been presented, but they were not honest enough to receive it and act on it.

This statement is parallel to what Jesus told the Pharisees after He had healed the blind man (John 9:39–41). They had to admit that Jesus had healed the man born blind, but they would not follow the evidence to its logical conclusion and put *their* trust in Him. Jesus told them that they were the ones who were blind! But since they admitted that they had seen a miracle, this made their sin even worse. They were not sinning in ignorance; they were sinning against a flood of light.

—*Be Transformed*, pages 67–68

8. Jesus explains that people will persecute because they "have not known the Father or me." And yet, the religious leaders heard the same message that Jesus' followers heard. Why is sinning "against a flood of light" worse than sinning in ignorance? (See 2 Peter 3:5.) Why, even with all the evidence presented them, did so many people choose not to believe? How is this true even today?

More to Consider: According to John 15:19, we are now of Christ and "out of the world." What does this mean in spiritual terms? How is it lived out in practical terms?

From the Commentary

For three years, Jesus had been with them to protect them from attack, but now He was about to leave them. He had told them this earlier in the evening (John 13:33), and Peter had asked Him where He was going (John 13:36). However, Peter's question revealed more concern about *himself* than about the Lord Jesus! Also, his question centered on the immediate, not the ultimate. It was necessary for Jesus to explain why it was important *for them* that He return to the Father.

The major reason, of course, is that the Holy Spirit might come to empower the church for life and witness. Also, the ascended Savior would be able to intercede for His people at the heavenly throne of grace. With all of their faults, the disciples dearly loved their Master, and it was difficult for them to grasp these new truths.

—Be Transformed, page 69

9. Why is it significant that the Spirit comes to the body of the church and not to the world? (See John 16:5–11.) How does the Holy Spirit come to the body of the church? What are some ways the Holy Spirit manifests Himself in the church today?

From the Commentary

> Our Lord was always careful to give His disciples the right amount of truth at the best time. This is always the mark of a great teacher. The Holy Spirit is our Teacher today, and He follows that same principle: He teaches us the truths we need to know, when we need them, and when we are ready to receive them.
>
> —*Be Transformed*, pages 71–72

10. Compare John 14:26 with 16:13. What does this comparison tell us about the way God arranged for the writing of the New Testament? Why is this important for us to know today?

Looking Inward

Take a moment to reflect on all that you've explored thus far in this study of John 15:1—16:16. Review your notes and answers and think about how each of these things matters in your life today.

Tips for Small Groups: To get the most out of this section, form pairs or trios and have group members take turns answering these questions. Be honest and as open as you can in this discussion, but most of all, be encouraging and supportive of others. Be sensitive to those who are going through particularly difficult times and don't press for people to speak if they're uncomfortable doing so.

11. In what ways do you see yourself as Jesus' friend? Why is that important to you? What are some ways that being Jesus' friend plays out in your faith life?

12. In what ways have you experienced hatred from the world? What was your response to that hatred? How can Jesus' words in the gospel of John help you to endure the world's hatred of Christians?

13. How do you see the Holy Spirit acting in your life today? In what ways does the Spirit act as Counselor for you? When do you most rely on the Spirit?

Going Forward

14. Think of one or two things that you have learned that you'd like to work on in the coming week. Remember that this is all about quality, not quantity. It's better to work on one specific area of life and do it well than to work on many and do poorly (or to be so overwhelmed that you simply don't try).

Do you need to learn how to handle persecution? Do you want to better understand the role of the Holy Spirit? Be specific. Go back through John 15:1—16:16 and put a star next to the phrase or verse that is most encouraging to you. Consider memorizing this verse.

Real-Life Application Ideas: Study what's currently happening to Christians in countries where they are persecuted. Look for practical ways you can respond to the needs of persecuted Christians. Then invite family members and small-group members to come together and pray for those who are still struggling to live out their faith under the threat of violence.

Seeking Help

15. Write a prayer below (or simply pray one in silence), inviting God to work on your mind and heart in those areas you've previously noted. Be honest about your desires and fears.

Notes for Small Groups:

- *Look for ways to put into practice the things you wrote in the Going Forward section. Talk with other group members about your ideas and commit to being accountable to one another.*

- *During the coming week, ask the Holy Spirit to continue to reveal truth to you from what you've read and studied.*

- *Before you start the next lesson, read John 16:16—17:26. For more in-depth lesson preparation, read chapters 5–6, "Let There Be Joy!" and "The Prayer of the Overcomer," in* Be Transformed.

An Emotional Time
(JOHN 16:16—17:26)

Before you begin ...
- *Pray for the Holy Spirit to reveal truth and wisdom as you go through this lesson.*
- *Read John 16:16—17:26. This lesson references chapters 5–6 in* Be Transformed. *It will be helpful for you to have your Bible and a copy of the commentary available as you work through this lesson.*

Getting Started

From the Commentary

John 16:16–33 concludes the Upper Room Discourse and deals primarily with the emotions of the disciples. They were sorrowing, they were confused about some of Jesus' teaching, and they were afraid. It is an encouragement to me to know that the disciples were real men with real problems, yet the Lord was able to use them. We sometimes get the false impression that these men

were different from us, especially endowed with spiritual
knowledge and courage, but such was not the case. They
were human!

—*Be Transformed,* page 77

1. Read John 16:20–22, 24, 33. What do these verses teach us about where
we find joy? How does grief turn to joy? In what ways has the "Ask and
you will receive" statement been misinterpreted (v. 24)? What do you think
Jesus meant by it?

More to Consider: There is a principle in John 16:16–22 that states:
God brings joy to our lives not by substitution but by transformation.
What does this transformation look like?

2. Choose one verse or phrase from John 16:16—17:26 that stands out to
you. This could be something you're intrigued by, something that makes
you uncomfortable, something that puzzles you, something that resonates
with you, or just something you want to examine further. Write that here.

Going Deeper

From the Commentary

> In John 16:16, Jesus announced that in a little while, they
> would not see Him; then, in a little while, they would see
> Him. It was a deliberately puzzling statement (John 16:25,
> He spoke in proverbs ["dark sayings"]), and the disciples
> did not understand. This also encourages me as I study
> my Bible and find statements that I cannot understand.
> Even the disciples had their hours of spiritual ignorance!
>
> —*Be Transformed*, page 79

3. What does Jesus mean in John 16:16? What "return" is He talking
about? Why do you think Jesus uses figurative language so often in His
teaching? What is the time that is coming when Jesus will speak plainly
about His Father (vv. 25–26)?

From the Commentary

> The central theme of John 16:23–28 is prayer: "Ask, and
> ye shall receive, that your joy may be full" (John 16:24). It
> is important to note that the text uses two different words
> for "ask," although they can be used interchangeably. The
> word used in John 16:19, 23a, and 26 means "to ask a
> question" or "to ask a request." It is used when someone
> makes a request of someone equal. The word translated
> "ask" in John 16:23b, 24, and 26b ("pray") means "to
> request something of a superior." This latter word was
> never used by Jesus in His prayer life because He is equal
> to the Father. We come as inferiors to God, asking for
> His blessing, but He came as the very Son of God, equal
> with the Father.
>
> —*Be Transformed*, pages 80–81

4. Why does Jesus turn His focus to prayer in John 16:23–28? How does
this fit in with the ongoing timeline for His own story? How does Jesus
define the process of prayer in these verses?

From the Commentary

In John 16:29–30, the disciples suddenly moved out of their spiritual stupor and made a tremendous affirmation of faith. First, they claimed to understand what He had been teaching them, though this claim was probably presumptuous, as their subsequent actions proved. They seemed unable to grasp the meaning of His promised resurrection. They were bewildered even after His resurrection as to the future of Israel (Acts 1:6ff.). I am not criticizing them, because we today have just as many blind spots when it comes to understanding His Word. All I am suggesting is that their affirmation was a bit presumptuous.

They not only affirmed their understanding, but they also affirmed their faith and assurance. "Now we are sure ... by this we believe." It was quite a statement of faith, and I believe the Lord accepted it. In His prayer recorded in the next chapter, Jesus told the Father about His disciples and reported on their spiritual condition (John 17:6–8). Certainly He knew their weaknesses, but He was quick to approve their growing evidences of faith and assurance.

—*Be Transformed*, page 83

5. Is it possible to have faith, understanding, and assurance and still fail the Lord? Explain. What do you think caused the sudden turn in the disciples' understanding (John 16:29–30)? What does this tell us about the disciples' relationship with Jesus prior to this moment? How is this

like or unlike the process Christians go through today in their pursuit of biblical truth?

From the Commentary

> Whether He prayed it in the upper room or en route to the garden, this much is sure: The prayer in John 17 is the greatest prayer ever prayed on earth and the greatest prayer recorded anywhere in Scripture. John 17 is certainly the "Holy of Holies" of the gospel record, and we must approach this chapter in a spirit of humility and worship. To think that we are privileged to listen in as God the Son converses with His Father just as He is about to give His life as a ransom for sinners!

> No matter what events occurred later that evening, this prayer makes it clear that Jesus was and is the Overcomer. He was not a "victim"; He was and is the Victor!

> —*Be Transformed*, page 89

6. Go through the prayer in John 17 and circle the things Jesus prays about for His disciples and all believers. How do these requests compare to the things He prays for Himself (vv. 1–5)?

From the Commentary

> Our Lord began this prayer by praying for Himself, but in praying for Himself, He was also praying for us. "A prayer for self is not by any means necessarily a selfish prayer," wrote Dr. R. A. Torrey, and an examination of Bible prayers shows that this is true. Our Lord's burden was the glory of God, and this glory would be realized in His finished work on the cross. The servant of God has every right to ask his Father for the help needed to glorify His name. "Hallowed be thy name" is the first petition in the Lord's Prayer (Matt. 6:9), and it is the first emphasis in this prayer.
>
> —*Be Transformed*, page 90

7. In what ways does John 17 reveal Jesus' burden? How is Jesus' prayer similar to the Lord's Prayer (Matt. 6)? What can this prayer teach us about how to pray today? What is the role of prayer in glorifying God?

More to Consider: Why is it significant that the word glory *is used so many times in Jesus' prayer? How does this word affect the theme and focus of the prayer?*

From the Commentary

"I have given them thy word" (John 17:14; and see v. 8). The Word of God is the gift of God to us. The Father gave the words to His Son (John 17:8), and the Son gave them to His disciples who, in turn, have passed them along to us as they were inspired by the Spirit (2 Tim. 3:16; 2 Peter 1:20–21). The Word is divine in origin, a precious gift from heaven. We must never take God's Word for granted, for those who are overcomers know the Word and how to use it in daily life.

—*Be Transformed*, page 96

8. How does the Word of God help us overcome the world? What does it mean to be in the world but not of it (17:14)?

From the History Books

Throughout the history of Judaism and Christianity, there have been groups that chose to remove themselves from the ebb and flow of the larger community. The Essenes were a Jewish religious group that practiced celibacy and asceticism and lived a communal lifestyle not that dissimilar from later Christian monastic living. They are perhaps best known because they are linked to the Dead Sea Scrolls (ancient manuscripts that included multiple copies of the Hebrew Bible), which some scholars believe were their library.

9. Why do some groups choose to separate themselves from society in order to practice their pursuit of God? How does this fall in line with Jesus' prayer for believers in John 17? What benefits can such seclusion provide to religious study, prayer, and spiritual growth?

From the Commentary

In John 17:20–26 our Lord focuses our attention on the future. He begins to pray for us who live today, for the whole church throughout all ages. He has already prayed about security and sanctity; now the burden of His prayer is *unity*. He is concerned that His people experience a spiritual unity that is like the oneness of the Father and the Son. Christians may belong to different fellowships, but they all belong to the Lord and to each other.

The disciples had often exhibited a spirit of selfishness, competition, and disunity, and this must have broken the Savior's heart. I wonder how He feels when He sees the condition of the church today! The Puritan preacher Thomas Brooks wrote: "Discord and division become no Christian. For wolves to worry the lambs is no wonder, but for one lamb to worry another, this is unnatural and monstrous."

—*Be Transformed*, pages 98–99

10. According to John 17, what is the basis for Christian unity? Why is disunity so common in churches today? What would Jesus say about the things that cause disunity? How can churches encourage and support unity today?

Looking Inward

Take a moment to reflect on all that you've explored thus far in this study of John 16:16—17:26. Review your notes and answers and think about how each of these things matters in your life today.

Tips for Small Groups: To get the most out of this section, form pairs or trios and have group members take turns answering these questions. Be honest and as open as you can in this discussion, but most of all, be encouraging and supportive of others. Be sensitive to those who are going through particularly difficult times and don't press for people to speak if they're uncomfortable doing so.

11. How might you have reacted to Jesus' message in the upper room (John 16)? Do you experience the joy that Jesus talks about in John 16:20–22, 24, 33? How have you interpreted the "Ask and you will receive" statement in verse 24?

12. What are some of the things that have perplexed you about Jesus' teaching? What are some of the things you have "finally understood" about His message? What are some things you're still wrestling with?

13. What role does prayer play in your daily life? How can the prayers in John 17 help you focus your prayer time?

Going Forward

14. Think of one or two things that you have learned that you'd like to work on in the coming week. Remember that this is all about quality, not quantity. It's better to work on one specific area of life and do it well than to work on many and do poorly (or to be so overwhelmed that you simply don't try).

Do you need to wrestle with questions you still have about Jesus' message? Do you want to learn more about how to pray? Be specific. Go back through John 16:16—17:26 and put a star next to the phrase or verse that is most encouraging to you. Consider memorizing this verse.

Real-Life Application Ideas: Spend some time reflecting on all that the disciples have gone through from the first time they met Jesus until the Upper Room Discourse that ends in John 17. Think about the ways you're like these disciples. Make a list of the characteristics that you and the disciples share (curiosity, uncertainty, boldness, etc.). Then reread the prayer in John 17, imagining yourself in the room with Jesus during that time. What do Jesus' words inspire you to do today? What practical action does Jesus' prayer prompt? Be encouraged and step forward in faith this week as you learn to live as Jesus' disciple.

Seeking Help

15. Write a prayer below (or simply pray one in silence), inviting God to work on your mind and heart in those areas you've previously noted. Be honest about your desires and fears.

Notes for Small Groups:

- *Look for ways to put into practice the things you wrote in the Going Forward section. Talk with other group members about your ideas and commit to being accountable to one another.*

- *During the coming week, ask the Holy Spirit to continue to reveal truth to you from what you've read and studied.*

- *Before you start the next lesson, read John 18:1— 19:16. For more in-depth lesson preparation, read chapters 7–8, "Guilt and Grace in the Garden" and "'Suffered under Pontius Pilate,'" in* Be Transformed.

Guilt and Grace
(JOHN 18:1—19:16)

Before you begin ...
- *Pray for the Holy Spirit to reveal truth and wisdom as you go through this lesson.*
- *Read John 18:1—19:16. This lesson references chapters 7–8 in* Be Transformed. *It will be helpful for you to have your Bible and a copy of the commentary available as you work through this lesson.*

Getting Started

From the Commentary

Perhaps the best way to see the truths in John 18:1–27, and grasp the lessons they convey, is to pay attention to the symbolism that is involved. John's gospel is saturated with symbols, some more obvious than others, and these symbols convey some important spiritual truths.

—*Be Transformed,* page 105

1. Read John 18:1. In what ways might the garden represent obedience or submission in this passage? Why do you think Jesus chose to go to the garden to pray? Now read John 18:2–11. How was Jesus' decision to go into the garden an act of obedience?

More to Consider: The name Gethsemane means "oil press." How was Jesus' experience in this place like being in an oil press?

2. Choose one verse or phrase from John 18:1—19:16 that stands out to you. This could be something you're intrigued by, something that makes you uncomfortable, something that puzzles you, something that resonates with you, or just something you want to examine further. Write that here.

Going Deeper

From the Commentary

> Jesus fully knew what lay before Him, yet He went to the garden in obedience to the Father's will. He left eight of the men near the entrance, and took Peter, James, and John and went to another part of the garden to pray (Matt. 26:36–46; Mark 14:32–42). His human soul longed for the kind of encouragement and companionship they could give Him at this critical hour, but alas, they went to sleep! It was easy for the men to boast about their devotion to Christ, but when the test came, they failed miserably. Before we judge them too severely, however, we had better examine our own hearts.
>
> —*Be Transformed*, page 107

3. What does John 18:1—19:16 tell us about the importance of obedience? What do we learn about Jesus' divinity during this section of Scripture? About His humanity? What lessons can we take from this today as we consider how to be Christ-followers?

More to Consider: Judas's kiss was one of the basest acts of treachery recorded in sacred or secular history. Why do you think God had orchestrated a kiss to be used in this way? What does this tell us about Judas? About betrayal?

From the Commentary

All of the disciples had courageously affirmed their devotion to Christ (Matt. 26:35), and Peter decided to prove it, so he quickly drew out a small sword and started to fight! He certainly misunderstood what Jesus had said about swords earlier that evening (Luke 22:35–38). He had warned them that from now on the situation would change, and men would treat them as transgressors. He was not suggesting that they use material swords to fight spiritual battles, but that they get a new mind-set and expect opposition and even danger. He had provided for them and protected them while He was with them on earth, but now He was returning to the Father. They would have to depend on the Holy Spirit and exercise wisdom. Peter apparently took His words literally and thought he was supposed to declare war!

—*Be Transformed*, page 109

4. Read John 18:10. How does Peter's sword represent rebellion? What mistakes did Peter make in drawing his sword? Why did he fail so miserably? How is this like or unlike the way Christians with good intentions fail today?

From Today's World

Modern parables about betrayal usually take the form of movies or television shows. You might even find specific references to "Judas's kiss" in some of these narratives. Often, when a character is betrayed, the movie or television show becomes a story about vengeance for that betrayal. In many cases, the one who has been betrayed ends up with some sort of victory over the betrayer. Obviously, Jesus' story has a much different narrative path.

5. Why is American culture fascinated by revenge? How might modern cinema reframe the story of Judas's betrayal to fall in line with this sort of thinking? In what ways did Jesus' obedience to His Father lead to a surprisingly different victory than revenge would have provided?

From the Commentary

> The drinking of a cup is often used in Scripture to illustrate experiencing suffering and sorrow. When Babylon captured Jerusalem, the city had "drunken the dregs of the cup of trembling" (Isa. 51:17). Jeremiah pictured God's wrath against the nations as the pouring out of a cup (Jer. 25:15–28). There is also a cup of consolation (Jer. 16:7) and the overflowing cup of joy (Ps. 23:5).

Jesus had compared His own sufferings to the drinking of a cup and the experiencing of a baptism (Matt. 20:22–23). When He instituted the supper, He compared the cup to His blood, shed for the remission of sins (Matt. 26:27–28). The image was a familiar one to His disciples, and it is not an unfamiliar image today.

—*Be Transformed*, page 111

6. What does it mean to "drink the cup" (John 18:11)? How is that phrase used even today?

From the Commentary

In the garden that night, you would find both guilt and grace. Peter was guilty of resisting God's will. Judas was guilty of the basest kind of treachery. The mob was guilty of rejecting the Son of God and treating Him as though He were the lowest kind of criminal.

But Jesus was gracious! Like King David, He crossed the Kidron, fully conscious that Judas was betraying Him. He went into the garden of Gethsemane surrendered to the Father's will. He healed Malchus's ear. He protected His disciples. He yielded Himself into the hands of sinners that He might suffer and die for us.

—*Be Transformed*, page 115

7. In what way does Jesus exemplify the idea of sacrifice in John 18:1–9? What is Peter's response to Jesus' statement? What does this tell us about Peter's continuing lack of understanding about what Jesus' role was?

From the Commentary

There were three stages in both the Jewish "trial" and the Roman "trial." After His arrest, Jesus was taken to the home of Annas and there interrogated informally (John 18:12–14, 19–23). Annas hoped to get information that would implicate Jesus as an enemy of the state. He wanted to prove that both His doctrine and His disciples were anti-Roman, for then He would be worthy of death.

Stage two of the Jewish trial took place before Caiaphas and whatever members of the Sanhedrin the high priest could assemble at that hour of the night (Matt. 26:57–68;

Mark 14:53–65). When Jesus confessed clearly that He was the Christ, the council found Him guilty of blasphemy and therefore, according to their law, worthy of death. However, it was necessary for the council to meet early the next morning and give their verdict, since it was not considered legal to try capital cases at night. So, stage three of the Jewish trial took place as early as possible, and the leaders condemned Jesus to death (Matt. 27:1; Luke 22:66–71).

—*Be Transformed*, pages 119–20

8. Review the three stages of Jesus' trial as noted in the *Be Transformed* excerpt. How do these compare to the legal process we know today? What is significant about the way Jesus answered the various charges (John 18:20–23, 34–37)? In what ways was Jesus still teaching throughout this process?

More to Consider: Read John 18:28–32 and Luke 23:2. In these verses, we learn that Jesus is charged with leading the nation astray, opposing paying tribute to Caesar and claiming to be the Jewish Messiah and king. Why are these charges unsupportable?

From the Commentary

> In John 18:37, Jesus explained who He is and what kind of kingdom belonged to Him. Pilate probably did not grasp the significance of these profound words, but we today can discern some of the meaning Jesus had in mind. He was "born," which indicates His humanity, but He also "came into the world," which indicates His deity. The fact that Jesus came "into the world" means that He had existed before His birth at Bethlehem, and this is an important and repeated truth in John's gospel (John 1:9–10; 3:17, 19; 9:39; 10:36; 12:46; 16:28; 17:18).

> But Jesus not only told Pilate of His origin; He also explained His ministry: to bear witness unto the truth. His was a spiritual kingdom of truth, and He won people to His cause, not through force, but through conviction and persuasion. He spoke the truth of God's Word, and all who were His people would respond to His call (see John 8:47; 10:27). Rome's weapon was the sword; but our Lord's weapon was the truth of God, the sword of the Spirit (Eph. 6:17).

> —*Be Transformed*, pages 123–24

9. Read John 18:37–38. Why does Pilate ask, "What is truth?" What does this passage tell us about the definition of "truth" according to the culture of the times? What does Pilate's question reveal about his perspective about the accusations made against Jesus?

From the Commentary

> The Romans and Greeks had numerous myths about the
> gods coming to earth as men (note Acts 14:8–13), so it is
> likely that Pilate responded to the phrase "Son of God"
> with these stories in mind. Already the governor had been
> impressed by the words and demeanor of our Lord; he
> had never met a prisoner like Him before. Was He indeed
> a god come to earth? Did He have supernatural powers?
> No wonder Pilate was starting to be afraid! Also, Pilate's
> wife had sent him a strange message that he should have
> nothing to do with Jesus (Matt. 27:19). Jesus had even
> come into her dreams!
>
> —*Be Transformed*, page 128

10. Read John 19:8–16. Why doesn't Jesus answer Pilate's questions in verse 9? How does verse 11 point toward an answer? Why does Pilate keep trying to set Jesus free? What ultimately is the reason he hands Jesus over to be crucified?

Looking Inward

Take a moment to reflect on all that you've explored thus far in this study of John 18:1—19:16. Review your notes and answers and think about how each of these things matters in your life today.

Tips for Small Groups: To get the most out of this section, form pairs or trios and have group members take turns answering these questions. Be honest and as open as you can in this discussion, but most of all, be encouraging and supportive of others. Be sensitive to those who are going through particularly difficult times and don't press for people to speak if they're uncomfortable doing so.

11. In what circumstances do you struggle with obeying God? What is at the core of this struggle? How can Jesus' sacrifice help you overcome your fears of pain or loss (or whatever is making obedience difficult)?

12. In what ways are you like or unlike Peter? What are some examples of "good intentions" you've had that ended in failure? What lessons did you learn from those circumstances? How do you know when it's right to act and when it's right to remain silent?

13. Think about a time when you betrayed someone. What prompted that action? How did you feel afterward? Did you ever resolve the situation? Why or why not? Now think about a time when you were betrayed. How did you react to that betrayal? What can you learn from Jesus' response to Judas that can help you deal with people who betray you?

Going Forward

14. Think of one or two things that you have learned that you'd like to work on in the coming week. Remember that this is all about quality, not quantity. It's better to work on one specific area of life and do it well than to work on many and do poorly (or to be so overwhelmed that you simply don't try).

Do you need to address a betrayal in your life? Do you need to ask for forgiveness for disobeying God during a difficult time? Be specific. Go back through John 18:1—19:16 and put a star next to the phrase or verse that is most encouraging to you. Consider memorizing this verse.

Real-Life Application Ideas: One of the most upsetting things to read in this passage of Scripture is Peter's denial of Christ. Take inventory of your relationships today with people who are nonbelievers. Do they know of your relationship with Christ? If not, why not? Would they be surprised to learn you are a believer? Think about the way you interact with others and how that reflects on your faith and commitment to Christ. If you uncover any disconnect between your behavior or words and your beliefs, consider practical steps that will help you live according to your faith so that you will not be ashamed to admit, "Yes, I am a believer," should the opportunity ever arise.

Seeking Help

15. Write a prayer below (or simply pray one in silence), inviting God to work on your mind and heart in those areas you've previously noted. Be honest about your desires and fears.

Notes for Small Groups:

- *Look for ways to put into practice the things you wrote in the Going Forward section. Talk with other group members about your ideas and commit to being accountable to one another.*

- *During the coming week, ask the Holy Spirit to continue to reveal truth to you from what you've read and studied.*

- *Before you start the next lesson, read John 19:17— 20:18. For more in-depth lesson preparation, read chapters 9–10, "'Even the Death of the Cross'" and "The Dawning of a New Day," in* Be Transformed.

The Cross
(JOHN 19:17—20:18)

Before you begin ...
- *Pray for the Holy Spirit to reveal truth and wisdom as you go through this lesson.*
- *Read John 19:17—20:18. This lesson references chapters 9–10 in* Be Transformed. *It will be helpful for you to have your Bible and a copy of the commentary available as you work through this lesson.*

Getting Started

From the Commentary

Pilate delivered Jesus to the chief priests, and they, with the help of the Roman soldiers, took Jesus to be crucified. "It was the most cruel and shameful of all punishments," said the Roman statesman-philosopher Cicero. "Let it never come near the body of a Roman citizen; nay, not even near his thoughts or eyes or ears."

Crucifixion probably had its origin among the Persians and Phoenicians, but it was the Romans who made special use of it. No Roman citizen could be crucified, though there were exceptions. This mode of capital punishment was reserved for the lowest kind of criminals, particularly those who promoted insurrection. Today, we think of the cross as a symbol of glory and victory, but in Pilate's day, the cross stood for the basest kind of rejection, shame, and suffering. It was Jesus who made the difference.

—*Be Transformed*, pages 135–36

1. Review John 19:17–27. Why do you think God allowed His Son to be killed by crucifixion, versus any other method? How might the decision to crucify Jesus have been felt by those who were not His followers? By His followers?

More to Consider: It was customary for a criminal to carry his cross, or at least the crossbeam, to the place of execution. Scripture doesn't tell us why Jesus didn't carry the cross (see Matt. 27:32). Do you think this

is an important missing detail? Why or why not? What are the possible
reasons that Jesus didn't carry the cross?

2. Choose one verse or phrase from John 19:17—20:18 that stands out to
you. This could be something you're intrigued by, something that makes
you uncomfortable, something that puzzles you, something that resonates
with you, or just something you want to examine further. Write that here.

Going Deeper

From the Commentary

> Jesus was crucified outside the city (Heb. 13:11–13)
> between two other victims, possibly associates of
> Barabbas. We do not know where our Savior's cross
> stood. There have been so many changes in the topog-
> raphy of Jerusalem since AD 70, when Titus and the
> Romans destroyed it, that it is impossible to determine
> accurately either our Lord's route to the cross or where the
> cross stood. Pilgrims to the Holy Land today are shown
> both the Church of the Holy Sepulcher and "Gordon's
> Calvary" near the garden tomb.

The Hebrew word *Golgotha* means "cranium, skull"; Calvary is the Latin equivalent. We are not told why it had this peculiar name. Certainly Jewish people would not permit unclean skulls to be left at a place of public execution! For that matter, the bodies (with heads intact) were usually disposed of by burial (if the victims had friends) or by throwing them on the public garbage dump. "Gordon's Calvary" does resemble a skull, but did the terrain look like that two thousand years ago?

—*Be Transformed*, page 137

3. Do you think there's any significance to the name of the place where Jesus was crucified? Why or why not? Why is it important to note that Jesus was crucified between two criminals? How does the place of Jesus' crucifixion add weight and meaning to the story?

From the Commentary

Our Lord knew what was going on; He was fully in control as He obeyed the Father's will. He had refused to drink the pain-deadening wine that was always offered to those about to be crucified (Matt. 27:34). In order to fulfill the Scriptures (Ps. 69:21), He said, "I thirst." He was enduring real physical suffering, for He had a real human body. He had just emerged from three hours of darkness when He felt the wrath of God and separation from God (Matt. 27:45–49). When you combine darkness, thirst, and isolation, you have—hell! There were physical reasons for His thirst (Ps. 22:15), but there were also spiritual reasons (Ps. 42:1–2).

—*Be Transformed*, page 139

4. What clues do we have that Jesus was fully aware of everything that was going on as He was being crucified? Why was it important for Jesus to refuse the wine? What is the point of noting that the soldiers divided Jesus' clothes?

From Today's World

One enduring legacy of the drama of Jesus' crucifixion has been the performance of "passion plays" over the centuries since His death and resurrection. Dating back many years, these recreations of the Passion Week have varied from simple enactments to elaborate productions. Today, many churches (especially Roman Catholic churches, but also a number of

Protestant congregations) produce their own versions of the passion play during the weeks leading up to Easter.

5. Why do you think passion plays continue to be popular? What is it about these reenactments that draws people—both believers and nonbelievers—to watch along as Jesus goes through the most painful and, ultimately, victorious week of His life on earth? How can these plays help believers grow closer to Christ?

From the Commentary

> Two groups of people were involved in our Lord's burial: the Roman soldiers (John 19:31–37) and the Jewish believers (John 19:38–42). It was not unusual for victims to remain on the cross in a lingering death, so the Jewish religious leaders did all they could to hasten the death of Jesus and the two thieves. However, our Lord was in control, and He dismissed His spirit at "the ninth hour," which was 3:00 p.m. (see Matt. 27:45–50). The last three "words from the cross" were spoken within a short period of time just before He laid down His life.
>
> —*Be Transformed*, page 142

6. Read John 19:28–37. Why does Jesus say, "It is finished" (v. 30)? What was finished? Read Exodus 12:46; Numbers 9:12; and Psalm 34:20. How do these verses line up with John 19:33? Now read Zechariah 12:10 and Revelation 1:7. How do these verses line up with John 19:34? Why would these two actions have been significant to the early believers?

From the Commentary

If the gospel of John were an ordinary biography, there would be no chapter 20. I am an incurable reader of biographies, and I notice that almost all of them conclude with the death and burial of the subject. I have yet to read one that describes the subject's resurrection from the dead! The fact that John continued his account and shared the excitement of the resurrection miracle is proof that Jesus Christ is not like any other man. He is, indeed, the Son of God.

The resurrection is an essential part of the gospel message (1 Cor. 15:1–8) and a key doctrine in the Christian faith. It proves that Jesus Christ is the Son of God (Acts 2:32–36; Rom. 1:4) and that His atoning work on the cross has been completed and is effective (Rom. 4:24–25).

The empty cross and the empty tomb are God's "receipts" telling us that the debt has been paid. Jesus Christ is not only the Savior, but He is also the Sanctifier (Rom. 6:4–10) and the Intercessor (Rom. 8:34). One day He shall return as Judge (Acts 17:30–31).

—*Be Transformed*, page 149

7. Read John 20 and 1 Corinthians 15:1–8. Why is the resurrection a key doctrine in the Christian faith? What does the resurrection prove? (See Acts 2:32–36; Rom. 1:4; 4:24–25; 6:4–10; 8:34.)

From the Commentary

The first witnesses of the resurrection of Christ were *believing women*. Among the Jews in that day, the testimony of women was not held in high regard. "It is better that the words of the law be burned," said the rabbis, "than be delivered to a woman." But these Christian women had a greater message than that of the law, for they knew that their Savior was alive.

Mary's faith was not extinguished; it was only eclipsed. The light was still there, but it was covered. Peter and John were in the same spiritual condition, but soon all three of them would move out of the shadows and into the light.

—*Be Transformed*, page 152

8. Review John 20:1–2. Why is it significant that the first witnesses of the resurrection were believing women? How might the story have played out had the first witnesses been men? What does the way in which Jesus revealed Himself to the believers tell us about Jesus? About the value of each group of believers? About Christians today?

From the Commentary

When John wrote this account, he used three different Greek words for *seeing*. In John 20:5, the verb simply means "to glance in, to look in." In John 20:6, the word means "to look carefully, to observe." The word *saw* in John 20:8 means "to perceive with intelligent comprehension." Their resurrection faith was now dawning!

Jesus compared Himself to Jonah (Matt. 12:40), and on two occasions clearly announced His resurrection after three days (Matt. 16:21; 20:19). On Thursday of His last week of ministry He again promised to be raised up and meet them in Galilee (Matt. 26:32; and see Luke 24:6–7).

—*Be Transformed*, page 153

9. Read John 2:19 (see also Matt. 16:21; 20:19; 26:32; 27:40, 63–64). Why were Jesus' followers so surprised that He had come back to life? What does this tell us about the followers' faith? How is this like or unlike some Christians' faith today?

From the Commentary

Why did Mary Magdalene not recognize the One for whom she was so earnestly searching? Jesus may have deliberately concealed Himself from her, as He would later do when He walked with the Emmaus disciples (Luke 24:13–32). It was still early and perhaps dark in that part of the garden. Her eyes were probably blinded by her tears as well.

All He had to do was to speak her name, and Mary immediately recognized Him.

—*Be Transformed*, page 156

10. In John 20:15, why does Jesus ask Mary, "Why are you crying?" Is it significant that all Jesus had to do was say her name and then Mary recognized Him? What implications does that have for us today?

Looking Inward

Take a moment to reflect on all that you've explored thus far in this study of John 19:17—20:18. Review your notes and answers and think about how each of these things matters in your life today.

Tips for Small Groups: To get the most out of this section, form pairs or trios and have group members take turns answering these questions. Be honest and as open as you can in this discussion, but most of all, be encouraging and supportive of others. Be sensitive to those who are going through particularly difficult times and don't press for people to speak if they're uncomfortable doing so.

11. What strikes you most about the manner in which Jesus was treated during the trials? Have you ever experienced anything similar—being accused of something that was not completely true? How did you deal with your accusers? How did Jesus deal with His accusers?

12. What aspect of Jesus' death troubles you most? In what ways does His death on the cross cause you to feel pain? In what ways does it bring you joy? What does it mean to you that Jesus took your place on the cross? How do you live out that truth in your daily walk?

13. What excites you most about the fact that Jesus rose from the dead? How does that fact affect your life? What is it about resurrection that gives you hope? What are some of the areas in your life where you long for resurrection? What role does your faith play in discovering that?

Going Forward

14. Think of one or two things that you have learned that you'd like to work on in the coming week. Remember that this is all about quality, not quantity. It's better to work on one specific area of life and do it well than to work on many and do poorly (or to be so overwhelmed that you simply don't try).

Do you want to better internalize the magnitude of what Jesus endured on the cross? Do you want to discover what Jesus' resurrection means to your daily life? Be specific. Go back through John 19:17—20:18 and put a star next to the phrase or verse that is most encouraging to you. Consider memorizing this verse.

Real-Life Application Ideas: Plan or attend a passion play next Easter season. When you go, allow yourself to imagine what it would truly have been like to witness Jesus' crucifixion and resurrection. Take time afterward to pray, thanking God for the gift of life that comes from His Son's great sacrifice.

Also, if you have nonbeliever friends who are seeking truth and are open to considering Christianity, a passion play might or might not be a good event for them to experience. You know your friends—so choose wisely and bring only those folks who understand what they're getting into (the brutality of the crucifixion can be difficult for many who don't know the joyous ending place).

Seeking Help

15. Write a prayer below (or simply pray one in silence), inviting God to work on your mind and heart in those areas you've previously noted. Be honest about your desires and fears.

Notes for Small Groups:

- *Look for ways to put into practice the things you wrote in the Going Forward section. Talk with other group members about your ideas and commit to being accountable to one another.*
- *During the coming week, ask the Holy Spirit to continue to reveal truth to you from what you've read and studied.*
- *Before you start the next lesson, read John 20:19— 21:25. For more in-depth lesson preparation, read chapters 11–12, "The Power of His Resurrection" and "Transformed to Serve," in* Be Transformed.

Resurrection and Transformation
(JOHN 20:19—21:25)

Before you begin ...
- *Pray for the Holy Spirit to reveal truth and wisdom as you go through this lesson.*
- *Read John 20:19—21:25. This lesson references chapters 11–12 in* Be Transformed. *It will be helpful for you to have your Bible and a copy of the commentary available as you work through this lesson.*

Getting Started

From the Commentary

Our Lord rested in the tomb on the Sabbath and arose from the dead on the first day of the week. Many people sincerely call Sunday "the Christian Sabbath," but Sunday is not the Sabbath day. The seventh day of the week, the Sabbath, commemorates God's finished work of creation (Gen. 2:1–3). The Lord's Day commemorates Christ's finished work of redemption, the "new creation." God the Father worked for six days and then rested. God the Son suffered on the cross for six hours and then rested.

God gave the Sabbath to Israel as a special "sign" that they belonged to Him (Ex. 20:8–11; 31:13–17; Neh. 9:14). The nation was to use that day for physical rest and refreshment both for man and beast, but for Israel, it was not commanded as a special day of assembly and worship. Unfortunately, the scribes and Pharisees added all kinds of restrictions to the Sabbath observance until it became a day of bondage instead of a day of blessing.

—*Be Transformed,* pages 163–64

1. Jesus observed the Sabbath even in the tomb. What does this teach us about the Sabbath's importance? How have Christians observed Sunday according to God's original intent for the Sabbath? In what ways have Christians misused the Sabbath? What place do you think Sabbath rest should have in our lives?

2. Choose one verse or phrase from John 20:19—21:25 that stands out to you. This could be something you're intrigued by, something that makes

you uncomfortable, something that puzzles you, something that resonates with you, or just something you want to examine further. Write that here.

Going Deeper

From the Commentary

> It must have given the men great joy to realize that, in spite of their many failures, their Lord was entrusting them with His Word and His work. They had forsaken Him and fled, but now He was sending them out to represent Him. Peter had denied Him three times, and yet in a few days, Peter would preach the Word (and accuse the Jews of denying Him—Acts 3:13–14!) and thousands would be saved.

> Jesus came to them and reassured them, but He also *enabled them* through the Holy Spirit. John 20:22 reminds us of Genesis 2:7, when God breathed life into the first man. In both Hebrew and Greek, the word for "breath" also means "spirit." The breath of God in the first creation meant physical life, and the breath of Jesus Christ in the new creation meant spiritual life. The believers would

receive the baptism of the Spirit at Pentecost and be empowered for ministry (Acts 1:4–5; 2:1–4). Apart from the filling of the Spirit, they could not go forth to witness effectively. The Spirit had dwelt *with* them in the person of Christ, but now the Spirit would be *in* them (John 14:17).

—*Be Transformed*, pages 166–67

3. In John 20:19–23, Jesus sends His disciples out as His representatives. In what ways are today's believers in the same situation as Jesus' disciples were right after His resurrection? What does this commissioning of imperfect, often clueless men teach us about the sort of people God uses to do His work? What encouragement can Christians today get from this passage?

From the Commentary

Why was Thomas not with the other disciples when they met on the evening of resurrection day? Was he so disappointed that he did not want to be with his friends? But when we are discouraged and defeated, we need our friends all the more! Solitude only feeds discouragement and helps it grow into self-pity, which is even worse.

Perhaps Thomas was afraid. But John 11:16 seems to indicate that he was basically a courageous man, willing to go to Judea and die with the Lord! John 14:5 reveals that Thomas was a spiritually minded man who wanted to know the truth and was not ashamed to ask questions. There seems to have been a "pessimistic" outlook in Thomas. We call him "Doubting Thomas," but Jesus did not rebuke him for his doubts.

—*Be Transformed*, page 168

4. Review John 20:26–28. Why is the manner in which Jesus responded to "Doubting Thomas" significant? For what did Jesus rebuke Thomas? What does this tell us about the difference between doubt and unbelief?

From Today's World

One of the biggest "sticking points" in the minds of nonbelievers is that they can't accept Jesus' resurrection. While people from many different religions (and even those who claim no religion) hold Jesus in high regard for His teaching (particularly His emphasis on loving your neighbor and taking care of the poor), they stop short of acknowledging that He was God and that He rose from the dead. Even some who claim to be Christians wrestle with this aspect of the gospel story.

5. Why is the resurrection difficult for some people to accept? Why isn't the resurrection impossible? What does the resurrection tell us about the manner in which God works? Is faith opposed to logic, or does it work alongside logic? Explain.

From the Commentary

John could not end his book without bringing the resurrection miracle to his own readers. We must not look at Thomas and the other disciples and envy them, as though the power of Christ's resurrection could never be experienced in our lives today. *That was why John wrote this gospel*—so that people in *every* age could know that Jesus is God and that faith in Him brings everlasting life.

—*Be Transformed*, page 171

6. Why is it not necessary to "see" Jesus as the disciples did in order to believe? In what ways is the gospel of John all about "believing"? (Skim through the entire book to see how many times John references the idea of "believing in Christ.") What place does faith, on the basis of evidence, have in John's gospel?

More to Consider: Respond to this statement—"Either Jesus was a madman, or He was deluded, or He was who He claimed to be."

From the Commentary

The average reader would conclude that John completed his book with the dramatic testimony of Thomas (John 20:28–31), and the reader would wonder why John added another chapter. The main reason is the apostle Peter, John's close associate in ministry (Acts 3:1). John did not want to end his gospel without telling his readers that Peter was restored to his apostleship.

—*Be Transformed*, page 177

7. Review John 21. How does this chapter help us to see why Peter is so prominent in the first chapters of Acts? In what ways does this chapter help to refute the rumor that John would live until the Lord's return (v. 23)? What other purposes would the gospel writer have had for including this chapter?

From the Commentary

After His resurrection, our Lord was sometimes not recognized (Luke 24:16; John 20:14), so it was that His disciples did not recognize Him when, at dawning, He appeared on the shore. His question expected a negative reply: "You have not caught anything to eat, have you?" Their reply was brief and perhaps a bit embarrassed: "No."

It was time for Jesus to take over the situation, just as He did when He called Peter into discipleship. He told them where to cast the net; they obeyed, and they caught 153 fish! The difference between success and failure was the width of the ship! We are never far from success when we permit Jesus to give the orders, and we are usually closer to success than we realize.

It was John who first realized that the stranger on the shore was their own Lord and Master. It was John who leaned on the Lord's breast at the table (John 13:23) and who stood by the cross when his Lord suffered and died (John 19:26). It is love that recognizes the Lord and shares that good news with others: "It is the Lord!"

—*Be Transformed*, page 179

8. Read John 21:1–8. What was Peter's reaction to realizing that Jesus was the stranger on the shore? How does this fit with his character? In what ways is this a contrast to the way he reacted in Luke 5:8?

From the Commentary

Peter and his Lord had already met privately and no doubt taken care of Peter's sins (Luke 24:34; 1 Cor. 15:5), but since Peter had denied the Lord *publicly,* it was important that there be a public restoration. Sin should be dealt with only to the extent that it is known. Private sins should be confessed in private, public sins in public. Since Peter had denied his Lord three times, Jesus asked him three personal questions. He also encouraged him by giving a threefold commission that restored Peter to his ministry.

—*Be Transformed*, page 181

9. What is the main theme of John 21:9–18? What did Jesus mean when He asked Peter, "Do you truly love me more than these?" Why did Jesus repeat His question of Peter two more times? What does this entire section teach us about love?

From the Commentary

Jesus had just spoken about Peter's life and ministry, and now He talks about Peter's death. This must have been a shock to Peter, to have the Lord discuss his death in such an open manner. No doubt Peter was rejoicing that he had been restored to fellowship and apostleship. Why bring up martyrdom?

The first time Jesus spoke about His own death, Peter had opposed it (Matt. 16:21ff.). Peter had even used his sword in the garden in a futile attempt to protect his Lord. Yet Peter had boasted he would die for the Lord Jesus! But when the pressure was on, Peter failed miserably. (You and I probably would have done worse!) Anyone who yields himself to serve the Lord must honestly confront this matter of death.

—Be Transformed, page 184

10. Respond to the following statement: "Anyone who yields himself to serve the Lord must honestly confront the matter of death." How is this illustrated in John 21:19–25? Why does Jesus single out Peter for this discussion?

Looking Inward

Take a moment to reflect on all that you've explored thus far in this study of John 20:19—21:25. Review your notes and answers and think about how each of these things matters in your life today.

Tips for Small Groups: To get the most out of this section, form pairs or trios and have group members take turns answering these questions. Be honest and as open as you can in this discussion, but most of all, be encouraging and supportive of others. Be sensitive to those who are going through particularly difficult times and don't press for people to speak if they're uncomfortable doing so.

11. Do you celebrate a Sabbath each week? If so, on what day? How do you treat your Sabbath day? In what ways are you treating it as Jesus did? If you're not giving the Sabbath its due, what steps can you take to honor that day?

12. Do you see yourself as having been "commissioned" as the disciples were after Jesus' resurrection? Explain. What does it mean, in practical terms, that Jesus has invited you to continue the work He began? How are you doing this today?

13. In what ways are you like "Doubting Thomas"? How do you deal with your doubts? Where do you turn to wrestle with them?

Going Forward

14. Think of one or two things that you have learned that you'd like to work on in the coming week. Remember that this is all about quality, not quantity. It's better to work on one specific area of life and do it well than to work on many and do poorly (or to be so overwhelmed that you simply don't try).

Do you need to reevaluate how you honor the Sabbath? Do you want to learn how you can better fulfill the commission of Christ? Be specific. Go back through John 20:19—21:25 and put a star next to the phrase or verse that is most encouraging to you. Consider memorizing this verse.

Real-Life Application Ideas: Jesus sent His followers out to serve as He had served. He told Peter to "feed my lambs." What does it mean to you to continue the ministry Jesus began? How are you doing this? Consider new ways you can teach and preach the good news to the people close to you (or even to strangers) and then go boldly forward to spread the gospel. Meanwhile, continue to study God's Word so that you may be prepared for all the challenges that will come your way as you serve the God of creation.

Seeking Help

15. Write a prayer below (or simply pray one in silence), inviting God to work on your mind and heart in those areas you've previously noted. Be honest about your desires and fears.

Notes for Small Groups:
- *Look for ways to put into practice the things you wrote in the Going Forward section. Talk with other group members about your ideas and commit to being accountable to one another.*
- *During the coming week, ask the Holy Spirit to continue to reveal truth to you from what you've read and studied.*

Summary and Review

Notes for Small Groups: This session is a summary and review of this book. Because of that, it is shorter than the previous lessons. If you are using this in a small-group setting, consider combining this lesson with a time of fellowship or a shared meal.

Before you begin ...
- *Pray for the Holy Spirit to reveal truth and wisdom as you go through this lesson.*
- *Briefly review the notes you made in the previous sessions. You will refer back to previous sections throughout this bonus lesson.*

Looking Back

1. Over the past twelve lessons, you've examined the gospel of John. What expectations did you bring to this study? In what ways were those expectations met?

2. What is the most significant personal discovery you've made from this study?

3. What surprised you most about Jesus' story as recorded in the gospel of John? What surprised you about the disciples and their relationship with Jesus?

Progress Report

4. Take a few moments to review the Going Forward sections of the previous lessons. How would you rate your progress for each of the things you chose to work on? What adjustments, if any, do you need to make to continue on the path toward spiritual maturity?

5. In what ways have you grown closer to Christ during this study? Take a moment to celebrate those things. Then think of areas where you feel you still need to grow and note those here. Make plans to revisit this study in a few weeks to review your growing faith.

Things to Pray About

6. John is a book about believing in Jesus. As you reflect on the words of this gospel, ask God to reveal to you those truths that you most need to hear. Revisit the book often and seek the Holy Spirit's guidance to gain a better understanding of what it means to be a Christ-follower.

7. The gospel of John is unique in tone compared to the other three gospels. What is it about this telling of Jesus' story that stands out to you most? How can John's telling shed new light on what you know about the other three gospels?

8. Whether you've been studying this in a small group or on your own, there are many other Christians working through the very same issues you discovered when examining the gospel of John. Take time to pray for each of them, that God would reveal truth, that the Holy Spirit would guide you, and that each person might grow in spiritual maturity according to God's will.

A Blessing of Encouragement

Studying the Bible is one of the best ways to learn how to be more like Christ. Thanks for taking this step. In closing, let this blessing precede you and follow you into the next week while you continue to marinate in God's Word:

May God light your path to greater understanding as you review the truths found in the gospel of John and consider how they can help you grow closer to Christ.

The "BE" series . . .

For years pastors and lay leaders have embraced Warren W. Wiersbe's very accessible commentary of the Bible through the individual "BE" series. Through the work of David C. Cook Global Mission, the "BE" series is part of a library of books made available to indigenous Christian workers. These are men and women who are called by God to grow the kingdom through their work with the local church worldwide. Here are a few of their remarks as to how Dr. Wiersbe's writings have benefited their ministry.

"Most Christian books I see are priced too high for me . . . I received a collection that included 12 Wiersbe commentaries a few months ago and I have read every one of them. I use them for my personal devotions every day and they are incredibly helpful for preparing sermons. The contribution David C. Cook is making to the church in India is amazing."

—Pastor E. M. Abraham, Hyderabad, India